FROM THE DOG'S MOUTH

BARKS, YELPS & GROWLS ABOUT POLITICS, JACKASSES AND BLOWHARDS, RELIGION, CHRISTIANS AND JEWS, MY CHOSEN PEOPLE, GAYS, STRAIGHTS, CHARLIE SHEEN, JOY BEHAR AND ANYTHING ELSE I WANT TO YAK ABOUT

MR. DARBY

PUBLISHED BY WAVECREST

To Gail Bell, a four-legs' best friend
and my twin angels, Livia and Augusta Carney

❧

CONTENTS

INTRODUCTION

I am Mr. Darby

Let me be upfront from first growl: I refer to my lord and master as Daddy or Dada because although he has never had a pet or raised two-legged kids, he has done his best to whip me into shape, make me abide by his rules and do what I am told. Sometimes I call him mon père or il mio papà, even simply Mister G. He and I have become co-healers in his practice as a therapist. He counsels thousands of men, women and children as an intuitive, using Carl Jung and astrology to wring the truth out of them, and to tell them what the world looks like through his lens.

Thank God Dada learned how to read my mind, or as his momma Maggie would say, "listen to me," so he could channel my thoughts for this book. And make no mistake about it — this is my book, not his. He will write as I dictate or there will be no book. More on that later.

His Eminence has gotten a lot easier to live with since he and I had a meeting of the mind. And what can I say about him without a scintilla of fabrication? He does care about others and he is a no-bull-sh*tter. Dada tells it like it is. He cuts a clear swath through the screwed up culture in which two-legs live.

As my fairy tale begins, once upon a time I lived in Bloomfield, Iowa. I was one of seven puppies, and I love the breeders who supervised my grand entrance. Millie the midwife said I am the most unlikely Wire Fox Terrier she has ever brought into the world because I was calmer and less rambunctious from day one. She and her husband put me up for sale on their web site, but then they decided they wanted to keep me because of my un-Wire Fox Terrier temperament. Daddy saw my picture before they could take me off the sales block — he said a voice of intuition told him to Google "Wire Fox Terrier" — and they decided to let him buy me. As Millie said to Daryl, "We are in the business of selling puppies, not raising them."

When mon père made that call to Millie, she told her husband Daryl that she liked him.

"He seems real nice," she said. "This Sedona gentleman seems like he would make a perfect parent for Darby."

That was even after Dada spilled the beans. He told her he was going to Egypt in February but he wanted to get a Wire Fox Terrier for his birthday in March. He said he was anxious about getting his first dog, and he wanted me to be housebroken.

"He really does not want his new dog to poo and pee in his house," Millie said. "He admitted that he was real 'anal' about these things. I promised him that when he got the new puppy that the dog would not make a mess indoors."

Ha! Lots of luck, Dada. It doesn't work that way. Daddy never got me on a routine and I spent the first year-and-a-half regularly ruining his snow white carpet. Man, was he cranky when he walked into the Great Room early some mornings to find my "Good morning, Dada" repository.

It's important for you to understand the back story about il mio papà before you hear what I have to say. It explains a lot.

He was raised in a single parent household with five other siblings. They did not have money to feed and care for a pet, so he never knew how to raise a dog. We four-leggeds talk amongst ourselves all the time about how many of our owners are unprepared for caring for an animal. Most of us canines are ill-equipped to give what two-legs are looking for, but there was something special about the match-up between me and Mister G.

You see, I'm as intuitive as my owner. I knew outright that he and I needed one another. I also knew he had the right stuff to make it work, but it was going to take every ounce of endurance we both could muster.

Mon père is an intuitive counselor who tracks stars — usually not Angelina Jolie or Brad Pitt (although he does advise some of the silver screen sort from time to time). He tracks the shiny, twinkling kind, the ones found against the black sky, to see what makes people tick.

He did my astrology before he bought me. I was born on October 5th which makes me an "even-Steven, fair and balanced puppy." At least that's what he tells everybody. I have the Moon in Sagittarius, which says that I am real independent. Dada doesn't always like that. Since he never had a pet, he is making up for it by wanting more love and affection and attention than my Moon in Sagittarius wants to give. But I'll talk about that when we get into how I became his therapist.

I should also tell you right off the bat that I have two invisible guides. Mon père calls the Great White Brotherhood of Light the 'hoods'. They not only give me the information I need to survive this ordeal, but they help both Dada and me grow. My intuition and these two spirits funnel me information and support my healing through this process. They don't want a lot written about them (unlike all the "Look at me! See how powerful I am!" two-legs who are supposed to be guiding and leading the Great Unwashed). My sky spooks work in silence and with invisibility. More than a few of these two-legged self-appointed gurus have hoodwinked the masses for a long time. One is known to sue anyone who disagrees with him or mentions his name in print. But he'll get his — like, when he downtrends faster than the speed of light and all he'll be left with are creditors! Just know that my own spirit guides are with me, just as all of you have spiritual guides and healers who track you.

These spirits help to let you know where other people are coming from, especially published authors and "talking heads" on TV. I wish that some of those big pieces of stuff in the spiritual world of books and hooey would 'fess up'. It seems to me that they have humongous egos — and I mean over the rainbow self-centeredness. What happened to servant leadership? Just asking.

Now here's the scoop on the book. The only way I would agree to write this eye-opener was if Dada butted out. I want to tell the story about him and me and how he learned a lot because I agreed to stay around to teach him. But this book is more than that. It's about how I see the world of two-legs' politics, religion, spirituality, the Afterlife and the Herelife. It's also about how big pieces of stuff — politicians, movie stars, social butterflies, and yeah, spiritual gurus — are getting too big for their britches. You are going to read a lot about how differently a four-legged looks at life than most of you two-leggeds.

I should also tell you that I've decided not to change the names of those I'm writing about. Let the chips fall where they are meant to show that none of the two-legged world is quite as well put together as they seem to be. That includes unlikeable and infamous sorts and warm and fuzzy and well-known people too. You'll have a lot of fun looking at the world as a dog sees it because we canines laugh our rear ends off at how sordid and silly humans are. Make no mistake, there are a lot of you that we four-leggeds love to hang out with. You will read about a few of those too.

Mon père thought that he was going to send me back to Iowa eight or ten times in the first three months I lived in his house. Wrong. It was me who put the idea in his noodle to send me back. But every time I got him to pick up the phone to call my original parents, I could sense his sadness. He really wanted us to work out. He just needed a lot of help. He needed to learn how the relationship could work. And that is what this relationship and this book is all about — how il mio papà learned to love something or someone without the fear of that person or thing walking out on him.

Sit back and read what I have to say, and I hope you like the pictures. Unlike mon père's professional photographs, mine are not air-brushed. No touch-up needed. By the time you read my truth and nothing but the truth version of my life with Dada, I will be all of three years-old and counting, so what you see is what you get.

Oh, and by the way, if you send me a question about your dog, I'm happy to answer it. My email address is in the back of the book. Or Twitter me and I will get back to you. Guess who's on Facebook? You have to know I have my own website.

I look forward to connecting with those of you who want a dog's point of view about what does and doesn't work with your pet — and what does and doesn't work with the rest of the world.

Before I forget it, publishers take a zillion years to get these books onto your Kindle or whatever 29th century technology you use to read the latest and greatest tomes. As you hang onto my every word and salivate with all suggestions I proffer, here's a non-threatening caveat: my book is not ancient history. It is the recent past. The value of looking back is to deter-mine what lies ahead. And this you can sure. Mr. Darby's world is so fresh, even when reflecting on yesterdays, that you will have a good time taking a peek at your world though the eyes of a four-legged Wire Fox Terrier and his better-than-he-used-to-be keeper.

1

DON'T JUDGE A DOG

From the dog's mouth, here's how things started out when I got to hotter-than-Hades Arizona.

My keeper loves to tell one and all that I made a beeline for him when I got out of my crate at the Phoenix Airport. Who did he think I would run to? That loco señora from Tijuana? I hate refried beans and English is my first and second language.

From the minute I was hugged and kissed by my keeper, I knew I was in for a long and torturous time with him. He was as needy as anyone I could imagine. But there was something about him that made the trip in the belly of the airplane worth it. I could tell he was all heart but with a need to control me. That would have to change.

Thank the stars above that his business partner Scott and Scott's then-girlfriend, now-wife Alison were with us. We went to some fancy shopping mall in Phoenix where I was on display, typical of what dog owners like to do with their pets.

The minute we got to our casa on the golf course, my keeper had bought all the paraphernalia: my water bowl and my food bowl. He had toys and a fence, which instinct told me was a retraining device to keep me from messing on his white carpet.

I went into his bedroom and saw a dog. After going back and forth trying to get this four-legged look-alike to play, I realized I was looking at myself in a mirror. Gosh, I had hoped for a canine buddy, but no such luck. All in all, I liked the joint but I knew that Dada and I were going to have a lot of adjusting to do.

Anyway, you need a taste of my daily routine, and a view of the two-leggeds and four-leggeds who are now part of my life.

THE EXTENDED FAMILY

Besides getting used to a new home, the layout and sniffing out the backyard, I was put in my crate a lot. Dada knew that dogs do not poo or pee in there but they will if they have free roam of the house. When I was free, I did it a lot.

Finally getting me on a schedule was tough; Daddy needed a lot of help in this department from Scott. Scott is the real deal and an absolute in-tune kind of guy that we dogs love.

The first week I was in Sedona, Scott, Alison, Daddy and I took a four-hour road trip to Tucson where Daddy was appearing at the Festival of Books on the overcrowded University of Arizona campus. Man, were there a lot of two-legged humans of all ages, shapes and sizes. While il principe was giving a lecture and autographing copies of his new book, Alison and Scott took me on a long walk. I was only 10 pounds, and all the gawkers were "oohing" and "aahing" over me. Every time I would take a leak they would clap like I had discovered a cure for cancer. But when I did a big poo all the lookers and smellers were gagging and I assure you there were no "oohs" and "aahs." There were a few "god, how gross!"

That night we went to a not-too-fancy hotel to sleep. Alison and Scott took me to their room because they knew how to treat a five-month-old pup. They had treats and water and food and a few toys for me (and them) to play with. Several times in the night they took me out to do my business. All the while his majesty was sound asleep in the next room.

On the way home the next day I was in the back seat with my new Daddy but I wanted to curl up in Alison's lap. I guess I ought to have been happy to get to know my new owner. If you think he's intuitive, you might want to pay closer attention to me. You see, I'm good at guessing what's going to happen before it happens, just like he is. (This is my way of letting you know that he and I had a war of words, deeds and actions up ahead.)

Scott and Alison played a game going back to Sedona. They had adopted a new puppy that they were picking up at the Sedona Humane Society that Sunday afternoon, and they were trying to decide what to name him. Whoever guessed closest to the exact time we would get home could name the dog. Alison liked the name Chaz but Scott wanted to name the Red Heeler Australian Shepherd Riggs. Scott got the exact time to the minute so they named the ball of fur Riggs. Riggs has become my best four-legged friend. We play together at the office all week, although Daddy doesn't work there. He prefers to see clients at our house.

Riggs' arrival at the Humane Society is a most harrowing story. A Native American construction worker from the reservation, or the Res, had Riggs and his sister in the back of his truck. In a box. No air holes. No water or food. The two four-week-old puppies were rolling around in their own feces. (That scene would have been enough to make my Dada throw up. He hates the mention of poo and has a hard time picking up mine. Then again, he brags that he has never changed a diaper, either). A tourist saw the pups, called the Humane Society and they seized the dogs and arrested their owner. Alison was a reporter for the local rag at the time and she wrote up their story. She was so taken with Riggs that she and Scott decided to adopt him. The Humane Society kept Riggs and his sister until they were six weeks old.

There are some other important characters to whom you need an introduction. Dada and Scott have been good friends with a family named Bell. Gail is a real looker and she loves me to pieces. Sometimes I wish that mon père would send me to her house for some R&R. Her husband David seems to be a big piece of stuff in advertising. Rumor has it that he is a great cook but he never invited me to dinner. They have a Wire Fox Terrier girlie girl named Curtsey, whom I met a couple of years ago in New York. She is bossy, but a real babe and lucky to crawl onto so many laps of luxury.

The Bells also have two two-legged children.

Andrew is their son. Scott and Daddy call him The Kid. He's tall, handsome and smart, a great tennis player and more fun than mon père. The Kid gets on the floor with me and we play like a dog and his owner should. He came to visit us last summer and mon père got jealous because I curled up on the sofa and slept with The Kid. But Andrew straightened him out. He told il principe in an email that my love was deep enough for him and Dada and a lot of other people. The Kid is going to be a famous writer or lawyer or both. If I have anything to do with it he will one day be president of the United States.

Last but not short of a dollar is Ashley Bell, who il principe calls Diva. She has long blond hair and is some looker. Bella Donna, another of Dada's names for her, sings like an angel. I think she's headed for The Metropolitan Opera and La Scala. She and her brother and mother founded an opera company Divaria which is touring in cities she thinks love opera. When she took me on a walk one day, I just know she fell in love and wanted to keep me for herself. But my lousy karma is to stay with Dada, so I dropped my ordinarily straight up tail and went home with him.

RIGGS, ME AND A DASH OR TWO OF TROUBLE

The reason for that long and exhausting story is that one night when I was about seven months old and Riggs was about two months-old, Scott and Alison kept me while The Kid and Gail and il mio papà went to the movies and dinner. Here's where I got into a lot of trouble. Riggs was a little fluff ball and I was all of 12 pounds. I tried all night to hump Riggs. Scott and Alison got so upset that they put me in my crate, where I belonged. You see, putting a dog in a crate is like making a rowdy two-legged kid stand in the corner and wear a dunce cap. Because Dada never had a dog, he came unglued and got huffy with Scott and Alison whenever they put me in the crate — this time because I wouldn't stop jumping all over their dog. His majesty ranted and raved and threatened because Scott and Alison would dare criticize the one and only, Dog Superior, Mr. Darby. That could have been the end of me and Scott and Alison and Riggs, but Daddy and Scott are "12 Steppers" so they know how to clear up a small spat that otherwise could have turned into World War III.

Riggs and I are in the office with Scott and Linda Monday through Friday and we play like prize-fighters sparring. When Riggs makes that growling sound and flashes those big fangs of his, I run right at him as if we were in a title fight. We go at each other over toys and bones but when Dada sashays into the office to offer us a treat, Riggs and I sit like two mild mannered sissies. And of course, despite the calm stature, Riggs snaps those killer jaws at the treat, nearly amputating Daddy's hand.

We even get to play outside in a landscaped cactus garden. Riggs is as smart as I am so we know not to raise our leg to pee on one of God's prickly plants.

One day, Riggs and I really wigged out a man who works next door to the office. The paranoid dude is also a retired Marine officer, who, unsolicited, likes to tell people so as often as Dada likes to say that "Mr. Darby is peerage." (Peerage means of noble birth for those of you with challenged vocabularies.) As Riggs and I romped, we engaged in what might have looked like a KISS concert. Anyway, the Marine asked Scott if Riggs and I were boy dogs. Scott said yes. "Then I guess they are homos because they are kissing," the flat-top numbskull said.

Well, folks, let me tell you that there are more gooters in the Marines than in a Rainbow Gay Parade. (The Urban Dictionary says that "gooter" stands for a gay hooter and it is used to refer to two men riding on the same side of the street, predominately in South Florida.)

Scott told the imbecile, "They're just dogs." The stiff upper lip veteran strutted off like a confused homophobe. But my gut tells me he knew just what I was thinking. Now I know why a homosexual gets beaten within an inch of his life by such as this Marine do-do. Because he is different. Because he loves another man. There were two gay penguins making the world crazy last week because they were supposedly queer amphibians. Finally some Republican clucker like Rick Santorum butch slapped them and now supposedly they are straight waddlers.

Dr. Oler, the vet, told my Daddy that when a dog is neutered or spayed, then a dog is just a dog. Not boy or girl, just a canine, period. We get together without danger of a boy dog getting a girl dog pregnant. What else happens — which two-legs could learn from us "fixed" animals — is that the knife accomplishes what mon père attempts to do. He tries to show clients how to integrate their shadows. Dada's theory, "discovered" by a man named Dr. Carl Jung, is that the reason humans, both men and women, have problems with one another is that their shadow, or invisible partner, is trying to make a man face his girl side and a woman her boy nature. In basic lingo, to achieve balance.

We canines are balanced from the moment we are surgically evened out. Too bad human beings can't have a procedure like that. It would make il principe's work a lot easier.

Then there's Riggs and me and the biggest backyard in Red Rock Country. My keeper had a landscaper redo the yard for us dogs to rough-house and poo and pee until our tongues were hanging out. But the way he carries on when Riggs and I dig a hole in the holy ground of this Better Homes and Gardens layout, you know all this was all about him and not just for my buddy and me. Scott kidded Dada unmercifullly until he gave us back our playground. Immediately we stopped digging up the manicured sod.

Riggs and I run around in that yard like there is no tomorrow. Scott tells everybody that I am the most fearless little rascal he's ever met. He says that I would cross enemy lines to piss off an uptight biddy or to Alpha male another dog. And yes, he's right.

When Scott brings me home to my house every afternoon around 3 p.m., Riggs and I both jump out of the car and pee. One afternoon, a fluff-and-puff bitch down the street, Honey Bear, was out on a walk with her mother. As soon as I finished with my business I took off running faster than a bat out of hell to get a little of that Yorkie-Poo sexy sizzler. Scott came roaring after me and when he did, he put me in the car and took me back to Dada.

You want to know what I think? Man, this dog's life ain't so bad, especially when I have Riggs in the morning and I get to sleep in Dada's bed at night. He really should change the monogram on the linens to read MD — Mr. Darby. After all I am peerage from Iowa becoming a full-fledged healer in Sedona, the Mecca of the Southwest.

2

TWO LEGS VERSUS FOUR LEGS

I love the way mon père tells a story. First off, the reason he has had so much grief about me is that he is as sedentary as I am a live wire. Case in point: his version of a slap-down on the sidewalk. He likes to say I wrapped my leash around his legs and tackled him. Truth? I saw a rabbit and went chasing after it. I happened to be on leash, the end of which was in Dada's hand. He thinks it is so amazing that I found my way home. I knew where I lived from day one.

Il mio papà is a name-caller at times. What he calls a runaway when the door is open just a tad is simply the nature of us Wires. We love to run and we should have been assigned to the Daniel Boones of the world since we love to hunt. Dada has a hissy fit when I start for the great outdoors, but it is in my blood to want to go out any chance I get.

He told Scott that one of the reasons he wanted a dog was to get back into exercising. Walking is the best way to drop a few pounds. Man does my lord and master need to lose a few. If he walks a half mile he thinks he's an Olympian. We need to walk two or three miles every day so mon père can turn blubber into muscle. I go on five-mile hikes with Scott and Alison and Riggs and I'm never winded. Okay, just a little, but I can keep up with them.

Walking is my chance to sniff out the territory. Dada ought to pay closer attention to why I want to be outdoors rooting around. Perhaps he doesn't get what the "fox" of my breed means. We Wire Fox Terriers like to chase and catch, well, foxes and other vermin. When I get outdoors I am in Fox Terrier heaven. He keeps me cooped up in the house too much. In the winter I have to stay indoors more than in the spring or summer. He should dress a little warmer so we can stay out longer. Sometimes it works, but other times not. When I say I'm intuitive, I'm not just whistling Dixie. I love the way Daddy hears me when I speak to him.

WHO'S SMARTER, A DOG OR HIS OWNER?

What is so wild about all this is that Dada thought humans were so much smarter than a runt of a dog. Boy, was he wrong.

Remember when he said the small voice of intuition told him to Google "Wire Fox Terrier?" That was my thought impression. When he opened the web site that had my picture on it, I said to him, "Hey, Mr. Sedona, send for me. I hear Red Rock Country is a bit woo-woo but beautiful. I'm ready to fly."

The trouble is that two-legged beings view dogs as their dependents. Thousands of books teach humans how to bond with their dog and how to make him mind. Dog owners want raising their pet to be simple and easy. But just as there are millions of types of two-legs, we canines have a wide range of "wills" and "won'ts" that are never addressed. For instance, no matter what the breed, dogs do not like to be controlled by their owners. We are looking for someone to accept us for who we are, not for who and what they need us to be.

My Dada is not the only person on the planet who can read me, but those who can are few and far between. The problem is that most people simply turn off their ability to communicate without words. Two-leggeds are under a spell to wide-spread egocentricity which cuts off their capacity to trust their intuition when it tries to express itself. What happened to il mio papà and me in short order was that he heard me when I spoke to him. He learned to catch the drift of what clients were trying to say to him in order to get his help even though they couldn't get the words out. Dada just knew; he intuited what they needed. I hear him say to his clients all the time, "I hear what you say but I know what you really mean." Thus, he began to vibe me and I sent him messages as well. Moving outside the box of communication will enhance how a dog and his keeper connect.

RULES AND DEREGULATIONS

From the very beginning there was a clash of wills between Mr. In-Charge and me. He always wanted me to poo and pee on command. (Let him try telling that to his fellow human beings.) And there's the eating thing, too.

"Eat, eat, eat," he'd bark at me the minute he put my food out. Of course, I rarely chowed-down when he wanted me to eat. I guess a lot of his ignorance comes from never having had a dog.

Dada could be mean. Oh, not boxcar murderer mean, but nasty enough. The maddest he ever got was when I wouldn't eat on his schedule.

For example: "Gobble your vittles. Eat, you rotten little terrier. This is my house and you will do as I say do or you're going back where you came from — and you can pay your own way back too." (He would push my face in the food, and of course I resisted by running from him. I'm faster.)

He barked some more. "I said eat and I mean eat or you will not get another bite of food for three days. I'll show you who's boss."

But then two minutes later he'd pick me up, trying to assure me that he loved me. His guilt overwhelmed his right to be the Alpha in our house. If I hadn't been able to read him, I would be a bit daffy.

Dada was most impatient about how I avoided my breakfast in the morning. More than a dozen times he turned beet red and raged at me if I had not cleaned my bowl by 7:30 a.m. Now, we are up at 5:00 a.m. so he can beat the rest of the world to first base, but I like to eat at 9 o'clock. Sure, there were times I ate right away when he put it in my bowl, but not because he was blowing a gasket. We did come to a meeting of the minds, but not because I suddenly started to eat when he commanded. I do like that he started dusting my dog food with liver and chicken and beef sausage bits. Yummy yum yum!

PUTTING CESAR MILLAN IN HIS PLACE AND OTHER MYTH BUSTERS

I will tell you exactly how Mister G started letting me chow down when I was hungry instead of just when he wanted me to. All the fancy dog trainers told him to pick my food bowl up after a few minutes if I didn't eat it, kind of with the attitude, "You'll show the dog who is alpha boss!"

Then, lo and behold Dada read an article in Time Magazine, "Dog Training and the Myth of Alpha-Male Dominance" in which the American Veterinary Association bashed Cesar Millan, that big britches from Hispaniola, the supposed high and mighty, king of king and lord of lords Dog Whisperer. According to AVA President Bonnie Beaver, know-it-all Cesar pins a dog on its back and holds it by the throat, which she said was downright cruel. (Dada was never under a swoon to the charlatan, thanks to the first time Dada saw him stroll through lover's lane with his pack of robotic mongrels). As a matter of fact Daddy and I think that when most people get famous they are on their way to Elvis' Heartbreak Hotel.

We are supposedly in the wolf pack line of evolution, but the founder of the Minnesota-based International Wolf Center, says, "Dog trainers have the wolf story all wrong, too." He further says, "Wolves in the wild actually live in nuclear families, not randomly assembled units, in which the mother and father are the pack leaders and their offspring's status is based on birth order." Don't you just love it when how we have been thinking for centuries gets turned on its ear?

This changed everything about how Dada I got along. This expert on canine behavior was like Dada's therapist friend Peggy who counsels her clients with patient-centered therapy. Letting a patient unravel his own crazy mixed-up life from childhood forward makes sense to me. Just like in nuclear families, canines must fight to make ourselves understood by our keepers.

Thank God for Time Magazine. Mon père stopped listening to all the so-called authorities and big pieces of stuff dogcrats (as he calls Dog Whisperers, trainers, vets, et al.) and started listening to me.

One fine day—almost like a Puccini moment in one of his grand operas —Daddy's 911-sized meltdowns about me not eating came to a screeching halt. (Can you hear the cymbals?) Amidst a colossal tirade a miracle happened. Humans talk about miracles all the time, but we dogs consider every minute of every day a miracle. Frustrated and filled to the brim with rage my keeper hit a wall. At the high note of his outburst he simply fell mute in mid-cry. He took a few deep breaths. Then he exhaled. His Napoleonic hunched shoulders relaxed. He went into the great room and lay down on the snowy white carpet and cried. He did not boo-hoo like one of Mrs. Hornblow's crybabies. But he cried out of frustration that he could not make me eat. I went over and licked his face and stretched out beside him. He turned his head and, nose-to-nose, toes-to-paws, looked into my eyes.

Here is what I said:

COMING TO TERMS WITH HIM AND ME

"Mister G, I know you are frustrated because I won't eat on your schedule. Well guess what? You know I have a Sagittarius Moon. I do things my way. How many times have you told a client that a Sagittarian is like a free range chicken, plucking and clucking anywhere and anytime they please? Well, sir, you have been describing me all this time and yet you never applied it to my eating habits.

"I know that you are trying hard to love me and you want me to love you. I do love you, but we dogs do not express affection like you humans. Humans seem to want something back in exchange for their love. You imply, 'If you love me Mr. Darby eat when I want you to eat.' It doesn't work like that in the animal kingdom. If you love me, you would let me eat when I am hungry, not when it is convenient for you. I know you better than you think I do. You want me to eat when you want me to eat to show me you're in charge. Which has nothing to do with unconditional love.

"Remember when you used to ask me why my eyes were wet? I was crying for you because I felt your sadness. I wept because I wanted you to be happy. But I am also frustrated because of how mad you get at me.

"Here's a compromise I think you can sign on for. Leave my food where I can get to it when I'm hungry. You were a lot smarter than all those smarty-pants dog trainers who told you to put the food away if I didn't eat within fifteen minutes. Instead you always left it near my water bowl. Good for you and me. Have a little patience with me. Living with you has tested my serenity, Mr. Drill Sergeant."

Dada stayed on the floor holding me close to him, me the little rascal, me the tougher-than-nails Wire Fox Terrier. He laughed until he cried and cried until he laughed out loud. We were this way for more than half an hour. He could sense what I was saying to him. You could tell without a shadow of a doubt (as Nancy Grace says as she hounds a murder suspect into the gas chamber) that he and I will never have another conversation about when I eat my food. (My poo is another story, and we'll get to that recurring theme before long.)

In sobriety circles, drunks talk about not quitting one minute before the miracle. Thank God Dada did not quit before I taught him patience and tolerance.

3

POO AND THE DOG PARK

In the beginning, Dada became most upset when dogs in the Dog Park would growl and chase me. He thought these ill-mannered rescues were vicious predators. He said as much to a few of the dog owners. One afternoon some big fat chick, who used to show her prissy Chihuahuas in dog shows, laughed out loud at Dada when he said, "Mr. Darby, stop sniffing that dog's rear end. That's filthy." She roared, "Oh my God, what's a dog to do? Sniff that area code, Mr. D." All the other two-legs let him know that dogs were just doing what dogs do — socializing and establishing who is Top Dog in the park.

He would have a meltdown if anyone put water in the kiddie pool because all of us dogs love to get wet and roll in the dirt. It would make il mio papà nuts because I was usually the ring leader. Water and dirt — yummy, yum, yum! Things have changed a little. Today he goes to the Dog Park with me and my only complaint is that he wants us to go home too early. He can swim and sun all day at his club but he wants me to be ready to tuck tail and leave within an hour.

But you have to give him credit. He's learning, and he's a lot more pleasant to be around. To tell the truth, I love him now and I think he knows it.

DUNCAN AND THE OLD RANGER

At a recent trip to the Dog Park, something unusual happened. As I said, Daddy freaks out if I take a mud bath. There is a phenomenon in Sedona that starts around the Fourth of July known as a monsoon. The grass gets soaked and mud-caked and there are dirty water puddles all over the park. It's something you just have to see, or for us dogs, to roll around in.

So that day, we went prancing in, me on leash and mon père hurrying me away from three dogs who were chasing tennis balls through muddy waters. When Daddy wants me to poo he doesn't want me to roll in the mud, chase balls or anything else. To him, this was a potty break.

Then a miracle happened. Daddy may have been touched by an animal angel. As if it were his daily custom, he leisurely let me off leash. I literally flew over to where a friendly dude I call the Old Ranger was throwing a frisbee across the football-length field. All of a sudden, out of nowhere, a Welsh Terrier named Duncan grabbed me by the neck with his teeth. I made sounds like I am dying — I learned this drama from Daddy and man, he sure can make a big deal out of nothing sometimes. Mon père pulled me from the jaws of perhaps instant death.

Now I have to give you some insights about Vince, owner of the terrier agir comme un fou (for the translation, hop a train with the hobos to the French Quarter in New Orleans and ask anyone in the Old Absinthe House. Open your yapper and say, "Pardon. Q'est-ce c'est ces mots?). He is the coach of the dog park—he's the "go-to" guy if you're a dog looking for a good time with a superman. Vince and Daddy seem to like one another. Vince throws the ball and whatever dogs are in the park chase them. I call him the Old Ranger but Daddy's best friend, Cathy — whom he calls Miss Israel or Super Jew — would call Vince a mensch.

I am not a blowhard or a braggart but I outran all the golden retrievers, Vince's Welsh Terrier and a big old ugly German Shepherd. The Old Ranger seems to favor me because he always says, "Go get it, Mr. Darby." Not that I need any encouragement as I have that winning streak in my gene pool. And of course I had to wallow in the mud to tease Daddy. He was hollering, "Mr. Darby, stay out of that mud if you know what's good for you." As Scott would say, my keeper was channeling his mother Maggie, who I've been told (time and time again) could be a real pisser. (I did see her picture once and all that "Sweet Jesus, loveliness and light" did not have me fooled. When you raise six brats like she did, especially with Daddy being one, I am sure she could raise holy hell if one of them disobeyed her.)

I always have a blast when the Dog Park is full of all breeds sniffing and chasing and having a good time. Vince always gives me a scratch on the back or says, "What a guy," to me and I love it. I keep wondering if that vicious terrier Duncan would trade places with me. Or as they say in the Army, Duncan could go TDY to our cottage on the golf course and I could hang with Vince. Daddy would whip Duncan into minding his Southern Baptist manners in a nanosecond..

I did not poo on this outing. Daddy always gets up in the morning to see if I left a smelly surprise on his white carpet under the table where he sits to work with clients. You see, we had company the night before I ran wild in the Dog Park.

Our visitors were Margot, a real fox, sassy and sexy and wearing a low cut dress, and her husband Tony, who was born in Belgium. Margot and my keeper did all the talking. I was so excited, going first to Dada and then to Tony. I stayed more with Tony because I heard them say he was a Pisces, like big piece of stuff Dada. When they got ready to leave, I wanted to go home with them. I flew out the door and tried to jump in their car. Margot had to collar me and take me back into my house. She is not only sassy and sexy, but she is a spoilsport. Drats, I guess they are either afraid of Daddy and what would happen to his temper if they tried to take me home, or else they have a dog already. And yes, Daddy told me when we went to bed that they had two dachshunds. Glory be. I would have a delicious time chewing on their ears as starters.

The next morning Daddy found a pile of my poo in four parts. I was so excited over meeting those two new people that I had to get up in the middle of the night to relieve myself. While I'm a very talented dog, I have not been able to jump high enough to unlock the sliding glass door. And holy St. Francis, he didn't scream at me. His exact words were, "I should have taken you out into the backyard after you met Margot and Tony because I knew you were excited."

Folks, you just read another reason why deep down I love my lord and master. He knows how to share responsibility with a dog that needs to poo.

That Schedule

We have an unbendable schedule at mi casa. I come home from the business office around three o'clock in the afternoon and il mio papà always asks if I brought home the bacon. He can be a smarty pants because he knows that Riggs and I are always playing and biting and yes, Signore Marine, kissing until we flop and nap. All play and no work and he and I like it that way.

Dada usually puts my dinner out when I get home. He works at his computer until his afternoon shower. (May I remind you that he refers to the computer as the anti-Christ. Yet he cannot stop using it. Go figure). Scott, who is like a son to him, says he always seems to be going into or getting out of the shower. Dada showers in the morning and before going to bed at night. He is from hillbilly Alabama where those God-fearing, Republican-voting rednecks take a bath once a week if at all. I have them beat. My groomer Diane bathes me twice a month when she strips and powder puffs me. Dada kisses me more than Riggs the day I am de-flead and fluffed — but that slows down until the next time I get groomed.

My first dog walker was a man named Bob. (Bob, by the way, left town more than a year ago and I've had a few new dog walkers. They're younger and more fun than adults). I would sit and stare at the door, waiting impatiently for Bob to arrive for my afternoon constitutional. We'd then go on a 45-minute walk, when I would poo and pee. God, anal Dada would always ask Bob, "Did Mr. Darby do his business?" The few times I didn't, mon père would go off the rails. He'd walk around the house asking me why I didn't poo. "Do you want more food?" he'd ask. Daddy is famous for holding his eliminations when he is on a plane or at the movies or in a restaurant. He even had a friend from North Carolina named Jim Bob who could never go to the bathroom in a public place. Mister G caught his phobia.

And a side note: After going on a walk with Bob, I hop on my Dada's bed and as he describes it, I scrunch my behind on a pillow on my side of the bed. I do like his bed, partly because I didn't like the alternative when it was first presented: "You can sleep in your crate or on 600-thread count Pratesi million-dollar sheets and pillows." (Mon père loves to tell the story of how Pemigio Pratesi started the sheet business in Vinci in Tuscany Italy in 1906. He goes nutso over anything Italian and is wont to say he'll take mafiosa over any other ethnic. I told you that Dada is more than eccentric!) The choice was a no-brainer so I have been on that fancy bed ever since.

LIVING BY GRACE

Here's a too-hot-to-handle saga of another trip to the Dog Park. Dada loves the fact that we dogs can do our business quicker and better when we smell other dogs. Anyway, I was sniffing and working myself up to potty, thrilling mon père with every whiff. All of a sudden I spotted this canine babe with chestnut skin and a tail wagging a million miles a minute with excitement at seeing me. I ran to her like a good ole boy from Powderly, Alabama, chasing a southern slut in a twirl skirt. Her name is Grace.

Wouldn't you know it? My Daddy knew hers, a chef named Alan. It seems that Alan's restaurant Fork in the Road recently closed. Fork in the Road was where Daddy and Scott took clients for their graduation dinners. Mister G is real picky about restaurants. His measuring stick for a great restaurant is Highlands Bar and Grill in Birmingham and Picholine in New York. He's been known to drop a few bucks for rack of lamb at Rene's in Tlaquepaque in Sedona. Yummy, yum, yum.

Grace was a Rhodesian Ridgeback, all of eight weeks old. She was frisky and she ran from me —and of course, I caught her every time and rolled her over and checked her area code. I had my paws all over her. What a honey. Already, I was in love. She may be too young for me, you say? Keep your two-legged opinions to yourself. When I come to the Dog Park it is open season for all bitches and me. Daddy asked Alan if Grace could come over to our yard for a play date. I'll show her a play date. She'll soon know that I may be neutered but I am still all man and then some.

I don't know a Rhodesian Ridgeback from a Heinz 57 variety slum dog. But I do know that whatever Grace's tendencies, I'll lick 'em and like 'em as long as they are hers. When we came home, Daddy looked up Rhodesian Ridgeback on the internet and here is what it said: "Red wheaten in color, ferocious in the hunt but at home she is calm, gentle, obedient and a good dog. They grow to be 60 to 80 pounds." Holy Toledo, Nellie. She is going to be a big one. Daddy always liked bigger women just like Tom Cruise. What I loved about the description is "ferocious in the hunt," especially if she is hunting for me. I think I dig ferocious. Fur will fly!

Speaking of bitches, I have been putting the thought in Daddy's head to get another Wire Fox Terrier, but a girly girl. He and his friends go to dinner and to movies. Ever so often they fly off to New York and hunt old digs in Egypt and go to the French Open in Paris. He's been bitching a lot lately about his Southern-based airline. Although he's a million-miler on this bucket of bolts, he is thinking of switching to another airline. I can tell him, but he won't listen: they are all crummy. They have too many hidden fees. Always late. All these hot air balloons will soon stuff so many people in smaller spaces that the obesity rate in the world had better fall or it will not be a pretty picture in the boxcars in the back. Anyway, his travel schedule may not allow for a sister act for me. Pity, I say.

4

TV, JOY AND STUPID PEOPLE

For as long as I could remember, mon père ate his dinner on a TV-tray watching one show at 6:00 o'clock in the evening: Joy Behar. She is a big-mouthed redhead with more opinions than a den of Beverly Hills ex-housewives trying to tell the Tri-Deltas how to catch a husband and take him for everything she can run away with.

Joy Behar is quick to curse and throw barbs at people she doesn't like, most of all Ann Coulter, a real mean-spirited potty-mouth blond. The yapper doesn't talk. She spews. Joy also hates that Aussie actor Mel Gibson who got into hot water with his wife and the press when he got some Russian chick pregnant. His wife finally divorced him and got a zillion dollar settlement. Joy would probably tar and feather him if she could. Oh, and Joy is Italian, which of course causes il mio papà to roll his eyes in a paroxysm of, pardon the pun, joy. The television maven, one of his majesty's favorite words, uses Italian words when she holds court.

After Joy Behar says, "Goodnight everybody," Dada reads for an hour and then turns out the light. That's when I hop out of the Italian finery and go to my own bed, which mon père got for me when I was done with the crate. If he gets up in the middle of the night to use the bathroom, he picks me up and takes me back to his bed and holds me tight. Soon enough, he turns his back to mine and goes back to sleep. I stay in bed until he wakes me at 5:00 o'clock with, "Wake up Mr. Darby, it is time to go potty and pee."

And that's how a dog with peerage and an ordinary garden-variety human ends and starts his days.

GLENN BECK NEEDS TO BE IN JUDGE JUDY'S COURT

One thing I like about il mio papà and our nightly bedtime ritual is that he no longer makes me lie under the covers like he used to. He stopped scrunching me in his arms and holding me tight. We recently watched the U.S. Open and saw Venus Williams and Roger Federer win their opening matches. I was catnapping and Dada scratched my back every now and again while he was glued to every swing of the racket from these two-legged stars. And when he turned out the light and we were close for a few minutes, he told me I could go to my own bed if I wanted to. I did, and jumped off that million dollar bed and those Pratesi sheets. I was fast asleep before he was.

It's time for me to weigh in on some of the yakety-yak-yak nonsense that is floating around terra firma. I was around during the Pony Express days when two-leggeds got their news a few weeks after the Indians lost another chunk of land and Abraham Lincoln got shot and killed by some nutcase. These days, humans get info in a nanosecond. Speed isn't always a good thing. What's wrong with turning things over in your mind? Why not give a thought impression time to breathe? Thank God my Dada didn't fly off the handle and ship me back to Iowa every time he got mad at me.

Oy vey, as the Jews lament. I would like to send Glenn Beck, a real television fruitcake, to Siberia. He rips and tears at any and everything liberal and humane and he orates and bloviates — an expression I heard from Bill O'Reilly, one of those other opinionated commentators on Fox, the most right-wing TV station on the air. Daddy actually declared "enough is enough from the insane asylum" so we don't even pause on that channel. He says it in such a sanctimonious voice that he sees devils and snakes crawling around Beck and O'Reilly and the rest of the mean-spirited commentators on Fox. Il mio papà believes that 2012 may mean the end of these irritating talking heads. What I can tell you is that I am glad that I can't be heard by anybody but Daddy because I would be on a lot of Hit Lists, locked up or "put to sleep" by these douche bags.

And then there is this issue of terrorism, which makes everybody from the four corners loonier than Olivia de Havilland in the snake pit. Two-legged types are trying to keep Muslims from building a mosque near "Ground Zero" in New York. God, I would think that more humane conscious two-leggeds would rather find peace in their souls and stop talking about 9/11.

Terrorists are like some dogs. All T's are a menace to human beings and some D's are a hazard to us dogs. But not everyone and not all Muslims are out to kill us patriots. They want to worship as they choose. Hate mongers spread this misinformation because they want everybody to live in fear, to get stirred up and to see a terrorist behind every tree. Live and let live. Worship as you like. Get out of the way so others can do the same. I love these bozos who preach First Amendment rights except when it interferes with their bully pulpit.

Why is it that when there is a disaster like Katrina, or Haiti or Pakistan, that everybody rallies around, never blinking an eye when the U.S. sends billions of greenbacks to help those in need? Everybody gets behind humanitarian causes. Disasters bring out the best in Democrats and Republicans, Christians, Catholics and Jews. But you let the president of the 50 states pass health care reform so that the poorest can get medical attention, or mention raising taxes to pay for better education across the board and the political demagogues want to impeach him. Go figure. From this four-legged point of view, somebody needs to get Judge Judy stirred up. I love it when she says, "I'm smarter than you on my dumbest day." When Daddy uses her line on his clients, the Great Unwashed make a shift, as do the defendants in Judge Judy's TV courtroom. From my view closer to the floor, there are a lot of mean and nasty people who think it is all about them and their almighty dollar. Soon all of this will change. Soon the other shoe will drop and then let's see who does what when there is greater parity, or as some would say, a redistribution of wealth.

On a lighter note, Scott and Alison and mon père went to the theater to see The Return of Nanny McPhee. Daddy kept repeating, "I'm Nanny

McPhee. Little `c,' big `P.'" I was trying to get their attention by vibing, "I'm Mr. Darby. Big `M,' big 'D,'" but nobody was paying me any mind.

And as always, we get back to poo. Mon père was having fits of joy and ecstasy when I made a big poo in the parking lot that same day. God, if I had known how Dada would get off on my poo I would strain to do it more often. No matter how much Scott tells him to quit getting mad at me if I don't go to the bathroom on a walk, Daddy still gets his underpants in a wad if I don't "go." Scott reprimands him, "How would you like it if someone was always saying, `When are you going to the bathroom?' `Why haven't you eliminated this morning, il principe?'" He is very anal but he is getting better.

CHARLIE SHEEN AS GOOFY GOOF

Oh brother, another ignoramus decided to take over the universe. Born September 3, 1965, his parents named him Carlos Irwin Estevez. Chuck Lorre, the producer of Two and 1/2 Men, hired him as Charlie Shine, I mean Sheen, and named his television character Charlie. Rumor has it that a therapist who shall remain nameless tried to hammer some sense into bonehead Charlie moons ago and the tiger blood "Winning" nixed the notion. Charlie's parents, Janet and Martin, are nicer than Aunt Bea and Andy on Mulberry RFD. Although mon père has been sober more than 32 years, Chuckles can't put together foty-eight hours one minute at a time. Daddy and I watched a couple of those dumb talk shows and man, is Piers Morgan another airhead suck-up artist. He was so thrilled to have the biggest loser on his show that pee-pee was rolling down Herr Morgan's lily-white legs.

During the Charlie reign of terror Daddy turned on the Joy Behar Show. Madam Behar was dishing about Signore Sheen. She suggested that a gaggle of Bellevue (the lock-up sanitarium in Gotham City, for the too sane to know) attendants snatch up Charlie Sheen between TV appearances and shackle him to a wall. For my two cents they should muzzle him—take away his privileges. She suggested Dr. Drew moderate the madness but I think Charlie needs the Divine Miss M, Bette Midler. Bette would either clear the air, clean out his pipes, teach him a few sober notes or f*ck him if he couldn't take a joke.

"Hail Mary, full of Grace.., blah, blah, blah.." Two-leggeds are proving every day how much we four-legs need a few barks and bites in the asylum of the puffed-up toady celebrities who have no clue which fork to pick up or when to stand for the national anthem. I am referring to the as*holes of all idiots, those Jenners and Kardashians, Kris and Bruce JJ's, Khloe, Kim and all those other KKK's. It is later than you think when a momma whores her daughter out with a sex tape and then goes to any length to extend their 15 minutes with a fake wedding to a douche bag. What were they thinking? In dog dicta: That's their problem. They can't think or won't about anything but the almighty dollah.

Now back to Charlie. He can't stop the diatribes and threats. With all due respect, I think Janet and Martin should not have spared the rod. This bitch needed a few years in isolation — no ice cream cones and no play dates.

When that bozo from network news showed the drug test from "Winning" it was all a big fat Henny Youngman "the joke is on Charlie" moment. Those who have been sober for five minutes know the dude is not straight and I suspect I mean that in the Biblical sense. Thank God the Twitter dingbat duffers jumped on the bandwagon in two minutes so the Sheen spewer locked and reloaded and came at network after network with "shock and awe." With the attention span of an ant, viewers eventually drove La Lunatic into a theatre near you and for too many pesos, you could watch a few more inane droppings from Charlie Bird. The latest breaking news is that Charlie Sheen will soon be back on television in some sort of rehab nonsense that will make Anderson Cooper's Ridiculist. Is all of this what Nikki Fink, the most-feared maven and creator of Deadline Hollywood, would call art imitating life? Or would she simply say, "Toldja!"

As Charles Laughton said in Witness for the Prosecution, produced by Arthur Hornblow, Jr., "Ladies and Gentlemen of the Jury, I rest my case."

HUBBA HUBBA HODA KOTB

On another night Daddy and I saw the beautiful and funny Egyptian, Hoda Kotb were on Joy Behar. We could not take our eyes from the screen or our ears from their voices. The two telegenics kibitzed and carried on like two yentas on a bus in Brooklyn. That Hoda is a fox. She evidently was married to a masher while she had life-threatening breast cancer surgery a couple of years ago. Joy, she of the anything-goes-mouth, pressed her for the sordid details.

Hoda laughed her onto a different subject: Kathie Lee Gifford. Behar was trying to get the Egyptian princess to badmouth Kathie Lee, but Hoda instead praised her to the hilt. The producers showed a film clip of Hoda and Kathie Lee appearing on camera on the Today show without makeup. Hoda looked terrific, Kathie Lee looked like a deer who had lost sight of the headlights. She needs to stay near Maybelline and those gay hairdressers and makeup artists. Principessa Lee looked real good for going-on-sixty, but she should never let anyone see her au naturel. But I will say this for La Gifford. She is funny and she can make herself the butt of her own jokes. That is a high form of 'don't take yourself too seriously.'

During one of the commercial breaks, Daddy mused that he thought Hoda and he and I had been together in Egypt during the dynasty of Ramses II. He swore he had a flash of that when Hoda was a correspondent on NBC Dateline. We flew to the computer and found out that Hoda was born August 9: a Leo. He creamed in his drawers. Dada was over the moon when he discovered that she had been a Tri-Delta at Virginia Tech. He knew some real bubble head sorority chicks when he was at the University of Alabama. His best friend was campus beauty and another Tri-Delta, (but a genius and an Elizabeth Taylor-lookalike) "Baba" Ruth Noble Golden who married Winston Groom, the author of Forrest Gump.

So when they came back on the air, Joy began to interrogate Hoda as if she were a murder suspect, pulling out all the details about her Egyptian background. Joy also said she didn't think Cleopatra looked like Liz Taylor but she thought Hoda might. Where does Joy Behar get this stuff? Daddy had great hopes that we'd get on The Joy Behar Show when this book jumps onto the New York Times Best Sellers List, but I dunno. She's a tough cookie. She might want to check to see if I'm Jewish. You know, circumcised. UPDATE: The Joy Behar Show has been cancelled. I guess we'll have to wait until she is reinstated or finds another gig somewhere else. I wonder if she's called Oprah at OWN?

What is so hysterical about Joy Behar is that she tries to convince everybody watching her show that all the girls on The View are good friends. Like

I am going to be suckered into believing that she and Elizabeth Hasselbeck are doing lunch. Or that she and Sherri Shepherd are the Dolly Sisters. I even have my doubts that she and Queen Barbara shuck and jive over tiny burgers at Swifty's, watering hole to the late and great Dominick Dunne and later and greater, Mrs. Arthur (Leonora) Hornblow, Jr. Joy Behar has a mind and mouth that engage faster than the snap-crackle-and-pop dialogue in The Social Network. A certain s*it-stirrer and Tea Partier Extraordinaire Andrew Breithbart said by remote broadcast on her show one night that Joy was "unhinged." Had he been live in her studio, the producers would have shown him to the service elevator right after the red light went out. He'd have been told never to walk on the same side of the street as Joy.

Mon père is definitely a Hoda Kotb fan. If he could figure out how to meet her naturally he would. He loathes people who suck up and turn cartwheels when they see a famous person. Hoda and he and I are Egyptians so that should count for something when it comes to chatting her up.

When we were done with The Joy Behar Show we stayed up and talked about all the women Daddy likes and who the world slobbers over. Il mio papà loves Reese Witherspoon but he can't stand Julia Roberts — that actress with the big mile-wide smile. It is something about that gargantuan mouth of hers and her constant narcissistic grin planted all over the front of magazines. His favorite of all times is Susan Sarandon. If anyone breathes a bad word about her, he goes ape. He loves Michelle Obama and Bishop Barbara King. He has a thing for black people.

But when the lights went out, the topic of conversation was the impending birth of Alison and Scott's twin girls, arriving on October 22. He knows their names but was sworn to secrecy from telling anyone except me. Never mind. By the time you read this Livia and Augusta will be headed toward their second birthday. Alison has gained so little weight that the Smithsonian Institute wants to have a wax dummy made of her at full term to show the world that you can bear two children and weigh less than Scarlett O'Hara did in Gone with the Wind.

Daddy, then, for some unknown reason, turned on the television to catch the late news. Lo and behold we saw pictures of the miners being rescued in Chile. It was so exciting and heartfelt to think that these 33 (the Christ number) miners were rescued alive after 69 days in the bowels of the earth.

Lo and behold both the mistress and the wife of one of the miners showed up at the rescue site. Who would have thought that such a miraculous event would be overshadowed by esposa y amante, or should I say, puta?

Sleepless in Sedona, we said our prayers to make us sleepy: "Now I lay me down to sleep, I pray thee Lord my soul to keep. If I should die before I wake, I pray for God my soul to take. If I should live for other days, I pray the Lord to guide my ways. God bless the twins and all our friends, two-leggeds and four-leggeds. Amen."

When we woke up the next morning, we saw the bloviator of all imbeciles, that Bill O'Reilly, on The View with Whoopi Goldberg, Elizabeth Hasselbeck, Sherri Shepherd, Joy Behar and Barbara Walters. He was making some silly ass points about why Barack Obama's popularity is sinking faster than the Titanic, and he laid it at the feet of Obama's position on approving of a Muslim mosque being built near the site of the Twin Towers. The former history teacher blathered and accused and got red in the face. When he began to marginalize Behar and Goldberg they walked off the show.

I promised Daddy that I would have nothing more to say about this man or any of his cronies. He called our cable service and cancelled Fox News. He just had the inane and stupid jabberwocky wiped off our televisions screen. Praise Allah and Jehovah and Ramakrishna.

Hallelujah! Hallelujah! Hallelujah!

GOOD THINGS DON'T ALWAYS LAST

Boo hoo. Miss Behar got the boot. HSN must have had a death threat from some big piece of stuff that she pissed off on air. Maybe the execs were afraid of what Mr. Darby would arf arf about when I got my air time.

No matter what you want to say about the bombshell, she was never at a loss for words. And she could bitch slap the best of them. She loved gays, Barry Manilow, the Osmonds, and a lot of comics and celebrities who were controversial. (As I said, mon père and I loathe these over-made-up wannabes. They are atrocious and give the two-legged population an even worse reputation than they deserve.)

If they put some idiot in her time slot I will personally pee all over their receivers. Joy will be remembered by me and il mio papà as the funniest stand-up broad we ever insisted on watching. She said she was too hyper to eat bon-bons and sit around the house filing her nails and waiting for the resurrection of Michael Jackson and Totie Fields. All I got to say is that she vibed me. I really thought I could go on her show when this book was published. I guess I'll have to suck up to Barbara Walters to get three minutes. With my luck they'll put me on as a warm-up act for somebody like Newt Gingrich. Girls, spare me. I know what Baba has in mind. She wants me to bite this politico on the ass so she can deny any liability. I'll show her liability. I'll storm her stage and look up her Nancy Northshore pinafore and see what junk she's hiding.

For now, I guess, TV will be all about the Animal Planet Channel Dada likes to watch. He's always taken in by stories about how abused dogs in New York and Miami and Philadelphia are rehabilitated for adoption by animal lovers. He loves to see a mangy, almost-dead dog come back to life through medical miracles and love and compassion from foster parents. Just like with his own practice as a therapist, Dada loves a happy-ending. So we watch Animal Rescue in Miami, in Houston, in New York and whatever other city they feature.

I would be short of a full tank if I did not let you know that we have discovered two new shows that leave Dada and me spine-tingling glued to the tube. When we saw the first episode of The Good Wife eyes rolled in both our heads over Julianna Margulies. Where did she come from? She glides in and out of court and usually wins her case because her writers make sure she does. Christine Baranski reminds me of a softer Mildred Pierce who never killed anybody. Baranski mows down the Attorney General's smart-ass prosecutors as if she edited the Harvard Law Review and sleeps every night to steady her nerves with that man who helped her get out of that indictment. Archie Panjabi is so crafty we need her in Sedona to get rid of a weird woman who won't pick up her dog's poo. Matt Czuchry acts so bitchy I wouldn't be surprised if he has a sex change written into his miserable life. All in all, Josh Charles knows how to bend the law to keep himself out of the slammer. You know what we hate? Bad television that appeals to those with an IQ of 45. When that trashy, not one iota of value, the Grammys preempts The Good Wife, it's bad for my life. Then another week it is the useless Super Bowl. But this week we are back in business with high legal drama at Lockhart & Gardner. Yummy, yum, yum.

Downton Abbey is another genius import from the British. They speak in that high fallutin' 'O, dear' tut-tut manner that we eat up. Lady Mary is enough to make the current Queen of England abdicate. The Mother Hen, Dame Maggie Smith can stir the fudge better than that fat lady in the kitchen can make trifle. (My Daddy met her once when he was still drinking. They guzzled a few bottles of très cher wine together. He still thinks she rearranged the stars he tracks) Dame Maggie is worth sitting through two hours because even with her snobby nose in the air, she is a ***** actor. She won an Emmy for playing her part. Wait until she wins another Oscar and then Dada can crow as if they were related.

5

Spirituality, Intuitiveness and Religion

What I find over the top is that human beings think we dogs are not nearly as smart as they are. I'm sure you've heard about how many words we can understand, and which kind is smarter than another, blah, blah, blah. No matter what breed, all of us canines are intuitive. We're also street smart and we know how to mind our ps and q's as well.

Mr. Darby Is Intuitive

There are a lot of unfounded and often-repeated facts about us four-legged creatures that amaze me. You see, mon père was doing all of us animals a favor when he took the time to read my mind and figure out that I was reading his. It is not words that are the basis of how we communicate, but attitudes and biases. Because he has spent eons reading people, Dada was primed to catch my drift. The problems he encountered were more of the "rules and regulations of how to be Alpha to his dog" that got him in trouble with me and me with him.

Let me tell you where most of the real intuition and mind-to-mind goes on between him and me: in his bed, which he insisted I sleep in when I was about eight months old. You could have floored me when he told me to get in his bed. I let him know to stay on his side of the bed. My bed time means rest my head on all the pillows so he and I make eye contact. We tend to our own mind for the longest time. And then he spoils the flow when he starts to stroke my coat and scratch my hind quarters. He coos, "This is Daddy's baby. Nobody loves you like I do." He already knows that I am crazy about a lot of people. I, unlike him, do not have an elitist bone in my body. Neither does Riggs or Scott or Alison. But we do our best connecting when he is quiet and we use eye contact to strike electric waves of non-verbal communication to one another. I think his tendency to want to talk "baby talk" is because he has lived alone for so long.

All of the things we do are learning curves for him. For me as well. There is never a one-way relationship between dogs and their human-owners. Some people act as if the dumb dog is just there to do what their owners want them to do. But that is not how things work in the animal kingdom.

Daddy gets this but I am going to lay it out for all of my followers. God uses animals, particularly dogs and horses, to get His messages across. The very fact that most people think we dogs can only growl and whimper to get what we want is short-changing the relationship potential. Thought impressions are more important than all the tricks people use to click connect with their dogs.

Speaking of tricks, it is not in a dog's best interest to have him roll over or dance on his hind legs to impress your friends. Kids don't like to be put on parade at parties. And they sure don't like to sit at the piano and make fools of themselves. Or worst of all, be forced to sing for their supper. Dogs don't like it either. We submit for the treats that follow the dog and pony show. It wouldn't hurt your relationship with your dog if you stopped all of this nonsense. Let him or her just be.

Past Lives, Present Tense

I hope you're giving second thoughts to the human idea of supremacy over animals. You see, we dumb animals even qualify to reincarnate.

Mon père writes and lectures and teaches about why we come back. Humans and animals. Where we start out before we are reborn. What happens when we die. His authority is backed up by the Vedanta Society, of which he is a devotee. Swami Swahananda, the big cheese of that order in the United States, is his guru. When he met Swami he had disdain for the term guru. Swahananda told him that a guru was a teacher like mon père. Daddy has been taught a lot by Swami Swahananda. By example. Through Vedas, Hindu scriptures like the Christian Holy Bible. Meditation is key to break with the illusion of the earth.

For those of you girdled by the better-than-thou syndrome, Vedanta teaches that God is in animals. So there. I know everything two-leggeds ever thought they knew. Dogs are created for the tradition of mind-to-mind communication. Read up on the subject. It was always the path to enlightenment in schools of thought in ancient Japan and China.

Dada reads to me a lot and we watch a lot of videos that back up what I already know. It rings true for me. I have had so many lives that my Akashic Record (for the uninitiated, an encyclopedia of all the lives you've ever lived and what you have done, good and bad, and what you need to atone for) is full of reference material. And, by the way, the best-kept secret on the Planet Earth is that animals play a role akin to Conte de Sainte Germaine. (For newcomers to Higher Consciousness, that spooky Frenchman has been variously described as a courtier, adventurer, charlatan, inventor, alchemist, pianist, violinist and an amateur composer. Most of all he is best known as someone who could dematerialize and show up somewhere else). Chew on that one, smarty pants!

Part of my mission with this book is to mess with your minds. So I decided that this is a perfect opportunity for one of us dogs to give our side of the story about reincarnation. Okay, stop muttering, "Oh, brother," under your breath. Daddy has known about how we all come back, animals and cats and birds, together or separately, to help us clean up the past and to stop acting like jackasses and make nice. You should have picked up a clue in this book you're holding in your hot little hands that he and I had to come back together because we both needed what only the one could give the other.

In case you were wondering if Daddy and I were in the Great Flood, saved two-by-two on the Ark with Noah, the answer is no. Rather, start with Daddy and me in North Africa. When he speaks in black churches mon père always says that he's a black man in a white man's skin. See. Soul memory helps him connect to his past in present time.

I was a favored canine in Egypt in his family three times and each time I was carrying a vibe to keep his majesty on the straight and narrow. But he kept losing the signal. In both Upper and Lower Egypt the dude in the short skirt wearing an over-the-top headdress was a floor flusher. (A floor flusher is a person, usually male, who pretends to have more money than they actually do as part of some twisted mating ritual. This will normally consist of owning a chariot they cannot afford, spending outrageous amounts of money at clubs and overdressing, usually in clothing pursuant to that of a hustler, mobster or high-rolling gambler portrayed on television.) He drank everything in sight morning, noon and night. The hooch got him drunk enough to say and do dangerous things. One time I had to calm him down when he was about to knock off his brother in order to sit at the head of the table. And inherit more than his share of fine art. He coveted the good silver. Il principe was a bad dude.

I'll set the scene for you. Egypt. Nineteenth Dynasty. A palace on the river Nile. Moses and the bulrushes. Multi-god worship. Politicians as bad as Ricky Perry and Newt Gingrich. Sinful sirens sold into slavery for sex (that would one day reincarnate as the Kardashians, Kloe, Kim and Kourtney). You get the backstory. His tribe started out as desert rats and ended up rolling in clover.

Enter his present-life momma Maggie, back then her name was Dorcas. His papa was senile and shiftless, so his momma fooled around with someone with three gold teeth and a lot more in a treasure chest. Dorcas was the first in a long line of gold diggers. Today they start out as trailer trash waiting tables in El Paso and then marry Texas billionaires in Houston. This past life was more thrilling and had more cinematic arcs than the Charlton Heston Paramount Pictures epic The Ten Commandments, in which phony Egyptians wore too much make-up and were bad actors.

Mon père's mère had been a slave girl and his father dealt in sheep and goats with a few camels that he rented near the Great Pyramid of Cheops. His Uncle Abdul couldn't keep his hands off his brother's wife Dorcas, so the two reprobates hitch-hiked on a felucca to parts unknown. I forgot to mention they stole il principe's daddy's box of gold. These two castaways got married after Dorcas got pregnant with little Samuel, who is now in his most current incarnation, my Daddy.

But it all ended just like with Romeo and Juliet. While living like fat cats in Abu Simbel with one of the 99 sons of Ramesses No. 2 they died on silk sheets drinking too much poisoned aphrodisiac which Abdul stole from a next-tent neighbor in Aswan.

Daddy and his three brothers, Ali, Calli and Joe fought over everything the two degenerates, Dorcas and Abdul left as an estate. The brothers didn't have to worry about the shenanigans of black sheep Samuel because he croaked from too much booze and too many broads when he was 35. I got left out in the cold. Those devilish brothers kicked sand in my puss and told me to beat it. When we died, we went back to the land of milk and honey (though there were no streets of gold that I ever saw). Daddy promised me that we would keep coming back until he learned to give me at least two square meals, clean water, a soft bed and a few treats and toys. And he would get sober. I never thought my butt would be sitting on Pratesi sheets, but he has finally kept his end of the bargain, and he is sober 32 years. He's done good.

My eyes roll in my head when Dada makes a three-act play out of all his past- life stories. For me, I stay in the present time and only wonder if the vet has succeeded in getting my lord and master to stop giving me too many treats. Like all canines, I live for treats, but Dr. Oler told Daddy a couple of weeks ago that I was two pounds over my "fighting weight." (You'd think I had to slim down for a boxing match or something.) So Daddy put a screeching halt to treats. Daddy has a short memory, and I guarantee you it is not Alzheimer's or even a senior moment. This seventy-something recovering Southern Baptist sinner is as sharp as a Swiss hunting knife. But I digress. I'll be scarfing up yummy-yum treats in no time. (At my latest vet appointment yesterday I weighed in at 20 pounds. Hallelujah! Hey, O High Holy One, where are the treats?)

Back to me, Mister G and our past lives. We were even together with Scott, Alison and Riggs in Italy and France. Dada and I both prefer Italy in this lifetime even though he hasn't taken me there yet. He hates to put me in a crate in the belly of the airplane and I hate it more. Maybe he and I will look at souvenir snapshots of his misadventures in the boot country instead of putting me through torture and possible death flying there, as happened recently to a poor pooch on a certain airline.

From life to life, the aforementioned motley crew moved around the old country like groveling gypsies. When the de'Medicis or the Borgias got too hard to handle, we skedaddled. The de'Medicis were too controlling and uppity and the Borgias were too cool with sleight of hand: they were known to slip poison in your cucina deliciosa.

Scott and Alison were in love (or lust) with someone else in this particular lifetime. Scott said to Alison, "Cara mia ti voglio bene," but she was betrothed to a rogue Castillian named Count Rosepelli. Their love and life ended unrequited, almost like Romeo and Juliet, without the poison. I was their dog and Riggs was my brother. Riggs and I, and Scott and Alison, for that matter, never fought, which is why Daddy is always asking them this lifetime, "Have you had a fight yet?" Now that Scott and Alison have reincarnated and are married, the twins came back into their lives to see what kind of parents they would be. Livia and Augusta had been their mother and father in that life time. Livia was the barrel-of-laughs mama, signora Balenciaga and the more serious-minded Augusta was papa, signore Balenciaga. It is no surprise that Augusta has the personality of Scott this lifetime and Livia is just like her mother Alison.

Scott was Daddy's illegitimate son. Daddy was a big piece of stuff in the Vatican and was not permitted to have children, but they all did anyway. Did you ever hear of Pope Alexander VI , father of Cesare and Lucretia Borgia? Bad dude and a real m*ther f*cker. Anyway, that is why Scott and Daddy had to reconnect this lifetime — so they could have a loving and peaceful and responsible relationship. My keeper owed him big-time and he has been making the karma right this time around.

What I love most about mon père is that he knows how to put all these past life dramas together. So do I. If you didn't like somebody in a past life you come back at war with them again. Love at "hello" says that you and that person will be compatible this lifetime. Actually, that is how the late and great Darling Hornblow described Daddy. She would ask about his agent Joan, and when Dada began to rhapsodize about Joan's brilliance, Darling would say, "Enough already about Saint Joan." Darling Hornblow was a real pisser.

In reincarnation, dogs change breeds like people change bloodlines. I started out as a hound dog and worked my way up into the high and mighty exalted lineage of Wire Fox Terrier. It is through finishing a lifetime with success that you get to move up the food chain. And it may hair-lip mon père when he reads this, but we are all the same. First a mangy old yeller and then a show dog. It happens. I'll talk about how stupid dog shows are later, but I'm just noting that I have gotten my peerage as perfecto as Daddy likes to brag.

Which brings me back to Red Rock Country. Sedona is to the spiritual seeker in the western world what Mecca is to the Hindu. Ever since a bigger-than-life (literally) psychic named Paige Bryant coined the word vortex to describe the spiritual energy in this valley of red rock, all the flakes and fools in the world have invaded Sedona looking for the meaning of life. When people ask Daddy if they should move to Sedona, he says, "Stay where you are. There is no spot where God is not." This is his way of keeping as many fruitcakes as possible out of town. I do know that Daddy and Scott refer to all these vivid imaginers as woo-woo. Now some woman has gone off and written a book called Eat Pray Love which Queen Oprah made a best seller. It was made into a movie that flopped. Let's see if India replaces Sedona as the destination in-place to spot the Holy Grail.

We were on a stroll in town one day and we ran into some weird woman dressed in an Islamic burka carrying a lapdog with the words "The Garden" shaved into its coat. Mon père nearly flipped out because he hates desecration of dogs more than Muslims loathe their ladies walking around showing skin. We checked around to see if they were filming a movie in the Land of the High and Mighty Spiritual Warriors of the Light and we discovered that Madam Self-Deluded got off a bus from Bakersfield, California. Daddy said he understood her intentions.

"Mr. Darby," he starts in his dramatic manner, "If you lived in Bakersfield, you would go anywhere the Greyhound bus could drop you because it ain't Mecca or Sedona anywhere near the city limits of B-town." Daddy finished his mocha latte and me my dish of water and we hurried home to watch Her Royal Highness of Television, Joy Behar.

GET A LIFE!

"The time has come," the Walrus said,

"To speak of many things:

Of shoes and ships and sealing wax,
Of cabbages and kings,
And why the sea is boiling hot.
And whether pigs have wings."
—Lewis Carroll, Through the Looking Glass

Enough of this idle chatter about the life and times of a Wire Fox Terrier and his sidekick, Daddy. You addle-brained two-legs have begun to act up and act out with such insanity and reprehensible thought impressions and actions that it is time once again for me to weigh in on the unspiritual and inhumane conditions of the about-to-be-late and not-so-great Planet Earth. If you don't watch your mouth and change your ways (I am speaking of the United States of America, which ain't so united) this terra firma will crumble and be blown away like the dustbowl during the Great Depression. Let the French and the Chinese and the Japanese and the Africans be held accountable to whomever they turn to in times of outrageous and blameful behavior. It's time you two-leggeds of the ole U.S. of A. started cleaning up your own backyard and stopped dissing the rest of the world.

For starters, where in the world did you descendants of the brave and courageous Pilgrims (now there's a core group you can be prouf of: they survived bad weather, bad attitudes, frustrations and insecurities, starvation, *and* still made peace with the Indians in order to get away from the tyranny of the King of England and his hooligans) decide that the government owes you a living? Most of you have been spending like there's no tomorrow. More than half the country decided to keep using their equity lines so they could live like the Rockefellers they weren't and still aren't. Any pea-brained half-wit could have figured out that housing was way overpriced. President Obama saved the economic structure of the country and now the blamers are throwing stones at him because the country is in the red. As if he had a good base to start with.

If you're looking for a Rainmaker or Miracle Worker look inside yourself. Be what you expect someone else to be or do for you. Would somebody give me the Big Book? Can we say the Serenity Prayer before I blow a gasket?

Listen up, mes amis of the Red, White and Blue. Contenders and pretenders. These blowhard jackasses are a reflection of what you are allowing to contaminate your think tank and unfeeling nerve endings. If your kids acted like this I hope you would make them wish they had never been born. So what do you do with these nutcases? You vote them in. What were you thinking? It's time to vote them out.

If you believe that this is a Christian nation, go to the Christian Science Reading Room and have one of the docents read you the riot-act. Under the first Amendment of the United States Constitution, it states that a person cannot "prohibit the free exercise of religion." Hence, a person cannot infringe on a person's right to practice their own preference of religion. Thus, the Constitution defends the freedom to worship as you please. Write that in cement and steel and read it to yourself until you get it through your fuzzy-wuzzy cerebellum.

Because I am as old a soul as any two-legs or four-legs breathing on the earth today, allow me to remind you of the History of the Decline and Fall of the Roman Empire. Read Edward Gibbon's account of how the greatest empire in the world failed miserably and why. The similarities to where we are today will astound you. Remember Buddha said, "Wake up!"

My two cents would say: Buckle down and get yourself out of the mess you made. Most two-leggeds are still looking for someone to solve all the ills that each of you created. They weep crocodile tears on the Other Side of Life when humans crave to have someone make their lives whole and financially well. The Good Book says, "For the love of money is the root of all evil." There is so much greed smeared across this country that the awakened dead would kill themselves at how idiotically and irresponsibly folks are acting.

Daddy and I were watching television and we heard that the rich among us are bitching about a raise in their taxes from 36 to 39 percent. The commentator said that in the Eisenhower era, the rich were taxed at 90 percent, and 70 percent under Nixon. (Note that both those presidents were supposedly staunch Republicans). When Clinton was president? It was 39 percent.

Because I am intuitive just like Daddy, I will give you my predictions for the United States of America:

1. Although the Republicans won the House and almost upended the Democrats in the Senate the last mid-term election, they will lose their grip in the House and the Democrats will keep hold of the Senate majority. If the Republicans win the House and Senate, it will be because the Democrats will have made their constituents crazier and angrier;
2. President Obama will win a second term;
3. Housing values will stay as low as they are until dumb nuts understand that this is a good savings deposit for retirement;
4. No matter what happens in the Mid-East, Israel will prevail;
5. If folks don't change, suicide rates will go up, birth rates will go down and life expectancies will plummet when old timers say, "We've had enough."
6. God will win in the end and life over there is still reality and here is still Reform School.

Dada just got home from a work trip to New York. He celebrated another birthday with the Bell Posse and Chao Liao and a blond named Maureen at the River Club. (You'd think they could have sent a private plane—I hate riding in the under-belly of Delta Air Lines or other bucket of bolts—so I could eat under the table and give Dada a few sloppy four-legged licks for his birthday, but n-o-o-o, MD was left off the list and out of luck). One night the core group, the Bells, Liao and il mio papà, were chomping on burgers and fries in the Library at the Regency Hotel and schmoozing about how to get the word out about my new book. One of the geniuses said that 'what From the Dog's Mouth needs was to know a BFF of President Obama.' The theory conjured up was that that friend could in turn tell il presidente that I, Signore Darby had predicted that Obama will win reelection in November. (Btw, a total no-brainer, even for a psychic four-legged canine with peerage like me).

As they were leaving the restaurant, eagle-eyed Kid Bell spotted a man who had been former White House Chief of Staff under President Obama. Sitting around the corner from the publicity pow-wow Dada and the gang had been having was Rahm Emanuel. They were as excited as if Christ Almighty had granted them one wish: the chance to boogie in the big tent.

Kid Bell: "Should we or shouldn't we?"

Il mio papà had written a book a few years ago that caused all and sundry to say all the time that such and so is 'a sign and a wonder.'

Here's the way mon père tells what happened and he's sticking to his story. Kid Bell, Chao and Dada walked right up to Rahm Emanuel's table and here's what was said.

Dada: "Mr. Mayor, may we have a word with you?"

Mr Mayor nods yes.

Dada: "My dog Mr. Darby has written a book. He predicts the reelection of President Obama. And besides, he barks and bitches about all the numbskull Republican nominees. We would like for you to read it. Maybe endorse it. Will you?"

His Assistant asked for Dada's business card; mon père did not have one to give him. (Why have them printed if you don't have one to give to the one who opens the door of opportunity when you knock? Duh, as Bart Simpson always says). Instead the Assistant gave Dada his card. "Send me the book and I will get it to the Mayor."

Since I believe in fair and balanced reporting (unlike the hot-air puff dragons on Fox News), I insisted that mon père and I erect and read Mayor Emanuel's astrological birth chart. Because I do not intend to tell my readers his planets in signs, I will let the world know that Mayor Rahm Emanuel and I have the same points of contact—we think alike, we express ourselves in the same way and we never take no for an answer if we are convinced that we are right.

Already I am prepared to go TDY to Chicago as First Dog, with Daddy's permission of course. And if Rahm Emanuel runs for higher office I will work in the trenches to see that he wins. This is a man who sees through steel, has the intuition of an all-seeing all-knowing mystic and can bore a hole through the opposition's platform. (Oh, and by the way, Mayor Emanuel, if you read this book and deign to give me an endorsement, I would love to wrestle Bo, the Obama's Portuguese Water Dog on the front lawn of the White House—riding upfront on Air Force One would put me over the rainbow for life.) Dada just said that with my tendencies to eliminate wherever I am, I would probably poo and pee on the highly-polished shoes of the Secret Service.

Sometimes I don't know when to stop and smell the roses because the stench of bad behavior is so overpowering. Then, the other night, Daddy tucked me in and gave me a lot of back scratches and held me tight. His spiel was how much he loved me and no matter what happens to him or to the world that we will be okay. Since I came into his life to help him make better choices he seems to love his life. You would have to know him to understand why his love means so much to me. It ain't easy being a dog and knowing what I know with the assignment I accepted before I reincarnated.

BARUCH ATAH ADONAI

We have a mezuzah beside our front entry. Nosy neighbors knock and ask if we're Jewish. And Daddy thought he left yentas behind in Alabama. Nope. They moved next-door.

Daddy says that he may not have been born a dyed-in-the-wool Jew but he wants God to bless this house like he does the kibbutz in Israel. He tells everybody who will listen that he was a rabbi in two past lives. The irony of his former rabbi-ness is that he would have converted to Judaism ages ago if a young rabbi named Scott had not told him he would have to give up Vedanta to be a Jew. G-d, ain't that a shame? Dada was ready to be a super Jew, proselytizing and everything and some smartass rabbi had to quash his desire to be a Hebrew man of God. He stuck with Vedanta, which says, "All paths that lead to God are right paths." So there, Rabbi Scott.

A lot of people ask mon père if he is Jewish and he answers, "Aren't we all?" When his mother Maggie died and his Jewish friends viewed the body, they said, "Momma's Jewish." He read a book once that said all of us are descended from the Twelve Tribes of Israel, even us canines. If the Baptists, a splinter group from Catholicism, knew this, there would be a lot of gnashing of teeth and breast beating. Those holy rollers think they are going to sit at the right hand of G-d — when there may not be a right hand or a left hand of G-d. If G-d is within each of us, why do we need to have to sit somewhere else? Just asking.

All of this Jewish business started when Dada met a gorgeous Barbra Streisand-loving, Bette Midler-acting Jewess named Cathy Friedman on her 40th birthday. I mentioned her in a previous chapter. Oy vey! The minute he laid eyes on her he began to call her "Miss Israel Civil Rights." Dada was raised in Birmingham, the center of a lot of dirt, guilt and shame around racism and anti-Semitism when he was young. He thinks of this especially because he had a colored lady — the euphemism for African-Americans when he was a boy — named Blanche, who ironed for his family in the post-Depression days, whom he wrote about in one of his books. He fell in love with Cathy at hello, even though she was and is still married to a happy-go-lucky, dog-loving dude named Paul. Paul cuddles nights with an oversized Rat Terrier named Bojangles. I can't wait to sink my teeth into that sausage hound!

Both were in one of mon père's Soul Mate lectures in Birmingham. (James Redfield who wrote The Celestine Prophecy, one of the world's most successful spiritual best sellers, was sitting ringside as well). Paul raised his hand when Daddy asked if anyone was married to their soul mate. Cathy screamed, "We're not soul mates," to which Paul piped in, "I thought he said cell mates." Everybody in the lecture laughed and that began mon père's more than 24-year relationship with Cathy and Paul and Judaism (and James Redfield).

I gotta tell you about Paul. Daddy's business partner Scott bonded with Paul like they were Lewis and Clark. The two brothers from different mothers were super buds from the moment they met because Scott concocted the best guacamole dip Paul had ever sunk his pearly-whites into, so they were tight-as-ticks evermore.

Paul calls Cathy the "hen," and he always roars with laughter when he does. She gets even with him when she tells all the Star of David wearers at Temple that she dare not interrupt Paul after 8 in the evening. He's dressed in his *heiso* sumo rassling outfit every night watching his fixed and unfair matches on television. Paul clutches that wiener of a dog of his and is under the spell of those gorillas on the mat as they fool him and millions of others into thinking they are having a legitimate contest rolling around in the ring. That's kind of hysterical, but not as funny as the time Paul was out of town and Cathy was chasing bats out of the house. These two are a pair. They remind il principe of the Bickering Bickersons, an old radio show from the 40's.

Cathy became Daddy's booking agent in Alabama. They are inseparable. When he was in Birmingham he would go to Temple on Friday nights.

Daddy was invited to bar- and bat-mitzvahs. When the cantor sang, mon père mimicked. My keeper put on the yarmulke and the kippah. If the rabbi asked the congregation to bring food for the poor, il mio papà brought bushels for the hungry. He loved to have dinner with all Cathy's Jewish friends, who in time became his clients and pals.

Once he went to Passover in Miami but he swore off that ritual, saying it was too long and he got too hungry. And the Praetorian guard wouldn't let il principe schmooze with Madonna and Demi Moore, despite the Beverly Hills version of Kabbalah preach the premise that we — movie stars and ordinary people — are all the same. Evidently we are, except when someone tries to suck up to Madonna or Demi. (At this time, I have no comment about Demi's recently reported stowaway in rehab. Let's see where that one lands.) Anyway, Daddy likes Temple Emanu-El better, a reform synagogue, where he can speak to all the big pieces of stuff like Donald Hess and Michael Pizitz. As mon père would say, "Ya gotta love those Jews!"

Cathy had an aunt who was right out of central casting. Aunt Florence lived in Palm Beach and was a true-blue snob of the first order. She had a yapper on her, which of course she overused. When Daddy met her years ago in a local hotel where she and other Jews were staying to attend a wedding, he asked her how she liked the hotel. She pursued her lips and said, "What a dump!" From that minute on he adored the ground she walked on and had to know everything Aunt Florence did or said. As the Jews would say, Aunt Florence was a tad meshuganah but Daddy loved her. She died at 101, kvetching and kvelling until the end.

Cathy has two daughters, Julie and Kate. When Kate was in junior high school, she took Daddy to her school classroom as Show and Tell. Of course, he talked about astrology. The teacher was a born-again Christian and was weeping and wailing in the cloak room while Dada told all the kids what astrological sign they were and what it meant. Mountain Brook is still talking about Daddy's anti-Christ episode. Kate grew up loving dogs and horses and she married a man named Josh Lourie, better looking than Brad Pitt with Elizabeth Taylor as his mother. Dada went to their wedding in Point Clear, Alabama and shucked and jived with all the brethren and sisters of Israel just like he'd had a bar mitzvah.

And then there is Julie, who has three adorable girls. She is divorced (Mister G. and Scott went to her wedding at Temple and a soiree afterwards that was fit for King Tut and his entourage), but I'll cover that tale in the next book. Julie is raising three stunning girls named Talia, Lila and Ava—what a trio, sure to be booked one day in Atlantic City in a revival of Gypsy. They'll cast Cathy as Momma Rose. When Talia was in a school production of Annie, the Musical, Cathy was at every performance with her backstage momma input and insights. Talia still thinks she's going to Hollywood and if Cathy has anything to do with it, she is already there.

The reason I am spending so much time talking about Cathy and the Jews is because I met Cathy when she and Paul came to Sedona. Cathy is a raving beauty and she inherited Aunt Florence's mouth. Cathy and Daddy would be in a dead-heat for who talks fastest and says the most. But my interest in her is that she is so caring and loving and giving. She is very involved in breast cancer philanthropy. When she hears that a friend of hers, or for that matter, a total stranger, has breast cancer, she is all over it. Short of administering the radiation or operating on the woman, she is so proactive that she puts the rest of womanhood to shame. You gotta love Cathy. Everything I have written and all the focus of this book is to get people to love one another, to live and let live, and when someone is in need, they should show up like Cathy does.

There is not a woman alive with good sense who will vote for Rick Santorum if he wins the Republican nomination for President of the United States. What Cathy is to women's rights he is a bad penny trying to undermine everything a woman holds sacred.

Daddy says she is an Aries, which makes her feisty and faster than a bullet train. She also has a Moon in Pisces, which makes her loving and caring. Whatever her signs and however she trips the light fantastic called life, I love her and I approve of all that she does because man oh man, does this hot and gorgeous Jew know how to live.

Writing about all things Jewish, one day recently an old biddy came into our yard and said she heard that I, Mr. Darby, was Jewish. She grabbed me and turned me over and looked at my uncircumcised pee-pee and said, "He's not Jewish." So I looked up her dress and yelped, "I don't know what she is, but it ain't pretty!"

Daddy goes off on anybody when they say s*it like, "He doesn't look Jewish." He can smell racism, anti-Semitism, homophobia and all other bigotries that are stinking up the planet and he doesn't let anyone get by with anything. Christians quote scripture but Daddy can give the statistics of all supposed heterosexual men who have a boyfriend and all married swan lake honeys who have a gal-pal on the side — and to the last quick draw, they are all homophobes. He is hardest on rednecks who use nasty epithets referring to blacks. Mon père is not so anti-Christian as he is in awe and shock how un-Christ-like most Christians are. And the dumbbell preachers and their hellfire and brimstone drive him up a tree. And if I could climb, I'd be at the top of the tallest redwood in California away from two-legged idiocy regarding closet sexuality.

My favorite saying is "You better be more concerned about where you're going when you die than putting too much stock into money, property and prestige while you are on earth." This four paws on the floor is looking ahead to where it matters most.

And as a footnote to Miss Israel. A few years ago Cathy was Person of the Year in Birmingham because she does so much good for so many people that the usual good-old-boys' club had to anoint her for her service. Daddy says that if Cathy ruled the world there would be peace on earth and we would all be saying "Mazel Tov."

As a sign-off after this rant here, let me say that I wish you all would check in with your insides and drop out of organized religions. You don't need a church or a temple to pray "peace on earth" constantly and do your part to make it happen. As Daddy and I like to say, "Change you to change the world."

6

DADDY'S CLIENTS AND FRIENDS

When I was seven months old I told my Dada that I did not want to be put in his bedroom with the door closed when he was working with clients. I let him know I was a healer. He seemed to hear me because from that day forward I was always with him and his patients. Once he had a pretty sweet lady from Canada who was afraid of dogs. She had been bitten by a cur when she was six years old. I somehow knew that already, so I laid my head on her feet under the table and told her, "I am here to heal you." She told mon père later that I got her over her fear of animals.

THE BLAME GAME

I was lying at the feet of one of Daddy's clients named Mike, who is part Mexican and part Irish. He got the loco rancheros from both sides of the DNA. One morning sitting at the long table by the window the two men were talking about blame. Lordy, don't stir me up. Daddy used blame on me when I was a puppy, and that turned into revelations for him. Now that Scott and Alison are having twin girls, they have promised Dada that he will learn to change diapers even if it nearly kills him. Sorry, back to blame.

Daddy reads the client's written homework and then comments on what has happened to him throughout his life.

You see, blaming others is the biggest black hole that exists on the planet Earth today. It predisposes that you don't have to take responsibility for your wrongdoing. You know, "The devil made me do it," as the Flip Wilson character Geraldine used to say to the judge. But Daddy knows his stuff. He knows you invite chaos into your life to teach you. He loves to crow, "There are no victims — never, ever — just volunteers." The worst whiners are women whose husbands have cheated, and men who say their wives are sluts. Somewhere in the ca-ca there were two of them doing the dance. No victims!

I want to make it known here and now that I am capable of influencing thought impressions. So while il mio papà and Mike were dissecting the harm that his parents and others had done to him, Dada dropped a bomb shell:

"Mike, you have been all these people before."

"You are telling me that I have been just like my three ex-wives?"

Sometime. Someplace. Somewhere. Each person had come into Mike's life so Mike could see indelibly and irrefutably his bad boy behavior. So he could change it. Daddy explained that when Mike faced his defects he would see these people as messengers from God. Then no one like them would ever come into his life again.

When Daddy first told Mike why he had attracted everyone including his family, Mike said he found reincarnation hard to swallow. "I was raised a Catholic," he said. Daddy thought, but didn't say, 'Sorry about that. Catholics have a lot to learn, including that there is a secret library in the Holy See that the Pope and his minions don't want any of us to see.. Century-old documents validate that we live life after life after life.'

With my vibing him, Mike gradually accepted past lives on faith. My contribution to the discussion was to make Mike more receptive to the notion that he had been around a lot of times. Because I had been under the table next to Mike for several days, I "opened him up" to the notion of reincarnation.

Back to blame. From my ankle-level view, I can tell you that humans are trained from the crib to the crypt to throw the blame onto someone else. It happens from childhood and follows two-leggeds to the bitter end.

So many people in this country are supposed to be Christians, but they're like 12-steppers who forgot to work all the steps. They quote scripture but don't practice what they preach.

And you want to know who hollers louder than a stuck pig? The rich man. The Christian Good Book also says, "It is easier for a camel to pass through the eye of a needle than for a rich man to enter the Kingdom of Heaven." And where is the Kingdom of Heaven? It is inside each of us, animals, aussi. I have it on good authority that God has assigned to the animal kingdom the task of getting two-leggeds to stop fighting everything and everybody, "To provide things honest in the sight of all men," and, "To live justly and to love mercy and to walk humbly with God." And how do we do this? With love. Do you think that there are those among humans who don't walk the talk? Woof, woof.

But all of this blame game leads to division and anger, which leads to skirmishes and eventually people go to war — over religion of all things for crying out loud. Imagine: "I'm gonna kill yo' ass in the name of God." Makes absolutely no sense. But what does make sense?

Dig this. Dig in and process. Talk amongst yourselves.

I worked with another of Daddy's clients. She was a nice lady who is really twisted about relationships, which happens to be my specialty. I figure if I can live with mon père without cracking up or running away from home, I can give this dame a leg-up with her husband. The problem is that she doesn't know whether she has a good deal with husband No. 3 or if she should keep looking. Speaking of looking, she is a real looker. I can tell beneath that Nancy Northshore personality that she is a real swinger. She could probably bust a few balls and make some dumb cluck bow before her nyloned leg. (Scusi, that was my last incarnation working a brothel in Singapore speaking.)

Rather than me placing blame, I have an admission to make. I did have a pile of poo accident last night. Dada nearly bit my head off when he had to clean it up. When we were out for the 6 a.m. elimination, he drove off and left me with a hundred crows waiting to peck out my beautiful brown eyes and make a holiday meal out of my hide. But Daddy is a softie so he came back and I jumped inside the car just ahead of the Alpha crow zeroing in on my butt.

Daddy found a healthier food for my diet, but switching over has caused digestive problems. A nervous stomach was what Daddy's mother used to call anything that caused her rat pack to be out of sorts. Blame and excuses. Excuses and blame.

So anyway, Daddy has to lay a little Sedona woo-woo on the whole she-bang — yes, the poo and the belly-ache — claiming that the Universe is trying to tell us something deep and meaningful about what's going on with me.

I got him to look into my mystical eyes that morning and I said to him, "Chill. O High Holy One. I am getting used to this new yummy food called Dr. G's but it will take a day or so to settle my stomach down. I can't seem to reach the knob on the door to take my upset outside. Because you were so wrapped up in the U.S. Tennis Open, you were not paying attention to my body language. So, during the night, when you were sound asleep, snoring like a buzz saw, I was unable to control my poo. I did go in three places because I was trying to get it all out of my system. Sorry about the mess but you say all the time that you'll take an accident here and there from me if I will always be in your life. So that's the truth and I'm sticking by it. Oh, it would help if you could let me out in the yard at night right before we turn in. Thanks for listening and hearing me."

So, my faithful readers and followers on Twitter, take those words of wisdom for your own doggies. Goodnight all. Sweet dreams.

AMADEUS

Dada likes two things more than anything: me and music, but not at the same time. Last night Scott and Alison and mon père watched the movie Amadeus, which according to them, won a lot of awards when it came out in theatres umpteen years ago.

Riggs and I were playing too rough and too loud for my keeper. He grabbed me in a half Nelson until I simmered down. Riggs and I started to watch the movie with the adults. I actually liked what I saw and heard. If you've never seen the film, it's about an old envious half-talented Italian geezer named Antonio Salieri (God, another Italian — no wonder Daddy almost fainted every time Salieri spoke in that wispy voice of his) who was obsessed with Mozart, a prodigy from the age of 4. To my way of thinking, Mozart was bored with his uptight life and decided to turn the channel and begin to write what he heard. I call that "being inspired." And just like in real time, the movie went black and we were unable to see what happened to the jealous old codger and Herr Mozart. The DVD broke. Rats.

When Riggs and Scott and Alison left our house, Daddy read a new book from his favorite author, Nelson DeMille, who he thinks is the funniest best-selling author writing. DeMille seems to be a wiseass and he always makes sure his main character, an FBI temp, always survives — even when he is fighting a terrorist.

While he was reading, I was remembering one of Daddy's and Scott and Alison's best friends, Joan. She died of breast cancer a few months ago and I miss her and her Cairn Terrier, Fenway. Fenway is a girl but not a girlie girl. You would have to look at her stuff underneath to see that she wasn't a boy. Fenway was so aggressive when I used to go to their house. For a bitch, she was mean as the dickens. All I wanted was for her to roll over and be sub-missive — but not Fenway. And Joan would always say, "Mr. Darby, you are in Fenway's house, so behave!" She doted on that dog like most guys do their "significant other".

What I loved most about Joan was that she could make Daddy laugh. As you might have noticed, he takes himself way too seriously. He thought she joked like a stand-up comic but she assured him that she delivered her best lines sitting down. Joan donated the money for the Sedona Dog Park, which she got the city to name after her pup. What an idea — a dog having a park named after her. Daddy is always telling Scott that if he croaks before I do, he is leaving all his money to Scott with the provision that he take me to live with him and Alison and Riggs, oh, and their twin girls. What a sweetheart deal! But to be honest, the way mon père spends money there won't be any left.

Humans have screwed up the economy so terribly that most folks don't have much money at all. Home values tanked and the stock market looks like it might take the patriots back into a Depression. But, hey, I didn't pick Daddy because he was a plutocrat. I wanted to live with him because I liked what he had inside — the good stuff that only I could bring out in him.

HARRIET AND DADDY

The other day the phone rang and Daddy put the phone on speaker so he could work and talk at the same time. He was jawing with his friend Harriet, a woman who started out as a client and became his friend, now going on 20 years. She is short and feisty like Daddy. I've seen pictures of her, but you could just tell from what she said on the phone that you don't mess with Harriet. Miss Harriet has the look and sound of putting you under a swoon. It was obvious that she can coo and woo with the best of them. She reminded me of Dada in a dress.

The long and short of the conversation was that she planned to come to Sedona to do some work with Daddy, and he invited her to stay with us in the guest room. You would think that room had been in Architectural Digest the way he goes on about what he's done to it. I tried taking a siesta in there once and I didn't like it. Too many pillows and throw rugs. Where do humans get all of these foofie ideas about what looks good? Dada loves to crow that it has its own private bath and can be locked from the inside, as if that should make any visitor feel safer or more welcome. Since I have lived with Daddy, more than three years, only one person has stayed in that room and I did not hear any raves when he left.

When Harriet visited, she and Daddy went to Sunday brunch at L'Auberge, one of the most expensive restaurants in the world. (It has only a few ratings on TripFinder. Wonder what that's about?)

Mon père said that Harriet had a nine-year-old dachshund but she decided not to bring him when she came to stay with us. Thank God for small favors as I do not dig those sausage dogs. I get hungry and want to chew on them when they come to the Dog Park. Daddy says that when I am in the park, I run the show and that I meet and greet and show the dogs out when they leave. Not exactly. It's just that I'm so cooped up in the casa and I like to run and play. I am still a growing boy. The Dog Park gives me jolts of energy. It's the only place where dogs outnumber people. I try to stay away from the benches under the portico where the owners sit and gossip. Listening to them is worse than getting a rabies shot. People really know how to bore the bejesus out of us dogs.

Dada and I sleep beneath a huge painting of an angel that he bought from Harriet's company, the Phoenix Art Group. (Actually, I sit on my pillow on my side of the bed and in the old days, after he fell asleep, I would hop into my tiny cashmere-lined bed. But not anymore. I love the California King his majesty and I share.)

When the world was still under its swoon of denial about the financial world, Harriet's company threw lavish parties, chock full of painted half-naked women who strolled around trying to get the partygoers in the mood to buy huge pieces of art. I know all of this because I heard Harriet and my keeper reminiscing about the 'good ole' days' — when the company could afford to throw these lavish excuses to sell art.

PINK AND BLUE

Daddy has been reading to me about the Breast Cancer Awareness shout-out in Magic City Birmingham for one of his best friends who is a breast cancer survivor, Carole Marcus Pizitz. Carole was honored for her good works to raise the consciousness about this dreaded disease and how much research dollars are needed to wipe it off the face of the earth. She is married to a big piece of stuff, Michael who owns Gus Meyer, a fancy schmancy upscale boutique emporium. (Dada has a few stories about Michael's Aunt Sylvia who was the Auntie Mame of the 60's in Gotham City. She used to take Mister G. to the ballet and opera and fancy dinners at a time when he could only afford to chow down at Horn & Hardart's, the automat—the cheapest place for twentysomethings to eat their grub in those days). Gus Meyer painted the walls of the store pink to throw the klieg lights on Breast Cancer Awareness. Mon pere says that when I turn four in the Fall he going to ask Mr. Big-Hearted Pizitz to throw me a birthday party to benefit homeless four-leggeds and those abused and abandoned by two-legged numbskulls. I saw a picture of Carole's Grand-Dog, Georgia a fluff and puff Havanese, the national dog of Cuba and a Bichon type. Georgia is known to have a spirited personality and a curious disposition. I'd cross state lines to show this cutie pie my disposition and more.

Dada loves to tell me priceless stories about Carole. He'd say something in his dramatic Leo voice, "Guess what?" And she would trill, "Oh-h-h, what?" And then they would fall out laughing. His favorite tale is how he told her about the woo-woo numbers, 666, on her automobile tag back in the 80s. She traded it in the next day. (For those not raised in the fear and dread of Southern Christianity, 666 is the supposed number of the anti-Christ. Not!) Carole has come to a lot of Daddy's sobriety parties. He loves to pick up photographs of her and ask people who know her, "Now how old was she in this picture?" Of course, she is ageless, even in bad lighting.

In case you are wondering if I lean politically, religiously and socially toward Judaism, yes, converted as charged. I got the bug from Daddy as he is always talking about Cathy and Paul, and Michael and Carole and her kids. He loves to say the Baruch and of course we have that mezuzah on our front door and Jerusalem relics all over the house. He foists Jewish Literacy on anyone who even hints of being curious or anti-Semitic.

Before I leave Mrs. Pizitz to live out her life on the highest hill on the richest private road in Mountain Brook or to soak up the sun from the verandah on her palatial beach cottage in Florida, I want to send her a zillion wet Mr. Darby kisses. Dada tells how she got her tuches (for you who do not speak Yiddish that means butt or backside) out of Memphis and down the road to the hamlet of red clay Magic City and tried to sell real estate. Then instead of being a slave to the lookey-loos she married the king of the hill, Michael Pizitz, and now she only owns real estate worth having.

Before I arf arf and say sayonara let me tell you that Dada knows her daughters Stephanie and Robin up close and personal. Once he was in Atlanta (Remember that huge scene in *Gone with the Wind* where Scarlett O'Hara rides in a wagon through the streets of Atlanta burning to the ground, wearing those green drapes she made into a dress, and says, "fiddle dah dee"?) with Stephanie and her future in-laws, the Selzers. Dada had dinner with them—not a kosher bite on the table—and they were schmoozing and yucking all night in an over-crowded, noisy bistro. Jason Seltzer got down on one knee, Stephanie said, "I do," and now they have two beautiful children, Kate and Dean. Central Casting will come calling on these two, sooner than later. I'll bet my last Confederate dollar that they will be big stars on or off the silver screen. And I can assure you that my Daddy had nothing to do with any of this.

Her other daughter Robin was smart enough, just like my keeper, to flee the Heart of Dixie and skedaddle over to what Mister G refers to as the freedom rider's dream destination, Aspen, Colorado. She is feisty and self-motivated—smater than a whip. One day while tending to her own business she met the man of her dreams, Chris Grey and they got married. Before too long the smartest soul who ever lived, Jaden was born and Robin and Chris have been trying to catch up with his genuis ever since.

I'd love to tell you everything I've heard about Michael Pizitz but I want that birthday party at Gus Meyer in October. You think I was born yesterday? When I see him I am going to run right up to him and ask if he wants to take me home on the highest hill in town to live with him and Carole and Georgia. I know which side of my bagel is buttered.

7

MORE LESSONS FOR TWO-LEGGEDS

Everybody has been on pins and needles, anxious to read about what I taught Daddy. He and I healed one another by what I did to provoke him and how he had to discipline me to raise a more behaved animal. It's simple, but you two-leggeds have trouble with plain Jane anything.

While we are on the subject of changing lives, you humans need to get a grip and be a little more discriminating. You buy all these books written by spiritual gurus by the carloads instead of teaching and learning amongst yourselves. I hate those "How to ..." holier-than-thou books. I don't care if I never hear another word from that big shot spiritual muckety-muck from Timbuktu. I don't have to name him — he knows who he is! It would take a translator from God Almighty to understand a word this supercilious phony is trying to say. Have you taken a gander at those Gucci glasses he's been wearing? And all you have to do to make yourself sicker is to see the suck-ups who are in a trance thanks to his eminence. Daddy says that this swami-wannbe would show up for the opening of a door. But men and women are trained in America to give their power away — and it always results in a cabal of authorities who clawed their way to the top and then set themselves up as the "go-to" paragons of truth. Ugh! Count me out!

Writing books has always been the exclusive right of two-legged smarty pants authors trying to impress everybody with how much smarter or cleverer or richer they are than the rest of the unpublished hoi polloi. But I've been around — don't forget that we dogs are reborn, too — and I know that take-no-prisoners-agents, pushy editors and bribery have a lot to do with what books humans are privileged to buy and thus which ones become Best Sellers. How do you know why one is a million seller and another an also ran? Answer: Only God knows. The Oprah Book Club was started to get more acolytes to grovel at her Highness' big feet. Along the way to her ego's exaltation she happened to have made a big noise about some books. Thank God Daddy didn't listen to one of his former agents who said he had to prove I could really talk before she would try to sell my book. Furthermore, she wanted a tape recorder to hear me reading what I wrote. Balderdash. Now you know why she's stuck between floors in her own incommunicativeness. She needs to look in the mirror and ask herself where she gets her information. One spiritual sister nearly buried her in crapola and never looked back to see if she was still breathing.

One of the things that bonds me with il mio papà most of all is that he never takes credit when people he works with change, and he will not take the blame when they go back to drinking or worse. In many ways, he's my kind of co-creator.

Human beings seem sillier and more gullible than us dogs. I have observed how people are either too fat or too skinny. What's that all about? Could it be that so many humans are feeding something neurotic and spiritually harmful to themselves? I know what skinny is — that's a Hollywood babe who think that she can never be too thin. Anorexia. Losing! Craziness.

Don't you find it nuts that mommas let their daughters get in a swoon over Hannah Montana, who is now known by some other name because she needs to up the age of her fan base? The minute daddies pick a sports hero for their sons to worship, the idolized athlete gets arrested for wife abuse or drug abuse or both — some even for murder. What happened to wanting your kid to grow up to be himself or herself and having parents who nurture who the good Lord created them to be? Just asking.

But then, publishers and talk shows on television — and you know that mon père and I watch a fair amount of TV — join the idiocy bandwagon and keep promoting diet books and how to get over what drives them to drink or drug or partake in their over-sexualized behavior. We animals have accepted that we come back to Earth to love and guide our owners, but human beings act as if money and name and fame are everything. Daddy is always poo-pooing Armageddon and the Apocalypse, but he better take a harder look at conditions of the planet Earth.

Yikes! I had better lighten up or you might start thinking I'm channeling Daddy.

What I am trying to underline and make bold (though my editor hates to overuse those tools) is that it is about time that all humans begin to take a closer look at what lessons they think they're learning but not applying to their lives. Get out of denial. It amazes me that these numbskulls think that someone knows something they don't. Is there something wrong with checking in with yourself so you can tell you what's right or what's not good for you? Stop looking to Gucci glasses for your answers.

Don't these Christian phonies know the Holy Book says, "The love of money is the root of all evil?" Where is walking the talk? What the heck. Daddy says that he has already sent in his vote for Obama, who wants to redistribute the wealth. As his friend Cathy Friedman would say, "Shalom."

GET A GRIP

Let me give an example of how two-leggeds get into their sturm und drang. I like to think of it as the dark and dangerous underbelly of the grin-and-bear-it cover-up. Daddy and I went to the Dog Park at 6:00 one morning for me to potty. He knows that (almost) without exception I will do my business. But not this morning. At five o'clock, before we headed out, he let me out into our garden while he showered. I did my business and went back in the house. Like most humans "of an age," Daddy forgot I'd been out already so we drove to the Dog Park.

So what did he do? I was slow to get back into the car — I was rooting around, lollygagging and getting whiffs of other dogs who left their essence behind for me to love and adore. All of a sudden, like shazam from a Superman comic book, mon père fell into a mood. (Or as Carl Jung would better express it, his shadow had him by the gonads). He dove deep, deep, down, down until his dark side hit bedrock.

"Alexandria" was having a snit. They can call it something innocuous as shadow if they want to, but what he switched on was mean and nasty and it tainted everything it touched. It specifically threw me, the dependent loving dog who thought il principe hung the stars and the moon, for the biggest loop your imagination can conger. So he jumps into our car and roars out of the Dog Park. I stood there like a knot on a log wondering, "What's gotten into him? Why did he leave me here?"

Now to be fair to Dada, as quickly as he became Mr. Hyde he shape-shifted into Dr Jekyll. He made amends for the scary part by saying, "This was not about you. It was all about me. My knee is still hurting from the surgery last week. I love you and you deserve better than the way I treated you." He kissed me and I accepted his amends by jumping in his lap to drive us home. He is from Alabama. "Stars fell on Alabama ... "

I told you this story because the world seems to have fallen into a dark-ness, and, inline Daddy, nobody is making amends by changing their behavior. So many people mask the wicked woman they are or the mali-cious man they have become. It is this tribal insanity that is spreading across the globe and which if no one discovers an antidote soon, there will be no deficit to deepen. The Divine will simply pull the plug and leave all the power brokers wondering where the Source went.

ELITISTS AS IDIOTS

Two-leggeds could learn a lot from us four-leggeds. Humans like to sepa-rate out socially, like the caste system in India. Riggs is a mixed breed rescue dog and I am hoity-toity upper crust. But we're the best of friends. But for humans, it's all about separation. Privileged families like to send their kids to the best schools. When they are toddlers, the upper crust keep their anointed chillun in schools that cater to the rich and infamous. Even with my pedigree, I would rather wrap my molars around Riggs' fury neck than eat a plate of steak and gravy. My groomer works with "show dogs" but I can tell she prefers to spruce me up than dunk and drip-dry those sissy bitches with blue ribbons and loving cups over their cribs.

Every time the Kid (Andrew Bell, in case you forgot) calls I get excited. He is so into what we four-legs think that I could bankroll him as President of the Animal Kingdom. The reason he is so jazzed about me and this book is that he thinks like I do, and he's the perfect example of a human who knows that pedigrees don't matter. When he was a freshman at this elitist middle school in Manhattan, he didn't like what he saw. He consulted with Daddy because he hated the snobby clique among his classmates. The Kid wanted to change to a multicultural school in Brooklyn. Mon père told him to get on a bus to see how long it would take him to get to school. After all, the other school was but a few blocks from his apartment. He got on the bus and it took 30 minutes. He called Daddy with the time frame and said, "I can do 30 minutes." So off he went, and he loved it, playing basketball and tennis and making good enough grades to get into Trinity College.

But what I love most about Andrew is that he knows how to play. And he knows how to love and care for all people, red and yellow, black and white. They are all precious in his sight. I had to teach Daddy to get on the floor, come out into the grassy area of our backyard or go to the Dog Park. Just to let go of everything and have a good time. The Kid was born to love life. He laughs at everything until he hears some bozo talk about the president being a socialist or when Madam Palin breaks out in ignorance, then the Kid can growl like I do when I see some big old hound dog acting like he owns my street.

But really, I have no problem with a dog, no matter where he comes from. If he was in a bitch's litter from a mongrel father, come on into my back yard. When some mutt with three legs shows up, I chase him as hard as I do my mixed-breed Riggs. We four-legs open our hearts to one and all, unlike two-legs who have so many pecking orders. I would not know who I was or what I could do if I had two legs. I'm not saying that there are no bad dogs. I know what happened to Michael Vick when he had dog fights for sicko gamblers to bet on, and there are a lot of two-legs who breed dogs to fight to the death. There are abused dogs who roam the streets to scavenger for survival. But more dogs than not are far more sensitive to how life needs to be lived than a lot of humans.

There are so many loose screws with two legs. The 2010 mid-term election was a good example of half-truths, mud-slinging and down-right vicious attacks on one's opponent. And for what prize? These nasty boys and girls wanted to represent two-legs in Congress, at any cost to their own dignity and sense of fair play, if most of them ever could be described thusly.

What really burns me up is how so many humans are selfish and don't seem to care that there are so many starving people right in their own back-yard.

Since we are in an election year and nobody wants to stop screaming long enough to care for the poor voters, the scuttlebutt is that the rich Republicans are like Marie Antoinette, the beheaded Queen of France during the French Revolution of 1789. When she said, "Let them eat cake," those Frenchies stormed the palace at Versailles and dragged her big behind to the sharpened razor known as the guillotine.

Kid Bell has it right. Blow the whistle and make every big bellied manipulative and controlling big piece of stuff be made to "'shut the *&^%& up" and let the people vote.

Things are going to get a lot better than they've been in a long, long time, if you ask me.

8

ARE WE HAVING FUN YET? WHY NOT?

Geez, I know that Mister G is no spring chicken but he seems to love to work all the time. He has little patience for those of us born to have fun. One of the main reasons God created four-legged "man's best friend" was to help human beings chill out and play. I can read il mio papà's mind: he loves it when Riggs and I have at it and chase and give each other love bites and seem to kiss. The truth be known, he and I are stealing each other's breath because we are so winded. Riggs and I are brothers, born in a different pack with different temperaments, but he and I bonded from day one because we love to have fun. We love each other.

ALL WORK AND NO PLAY

As you start to read this section I suppose you are wondering what could Mr. Darby teach his keeper about strolling down the street or a walk in the park? If you knew him like I do, you would not ask that question. He is always in a hurry. You dog owners know that you can't rush your poodle or your retriever. Dogs like to walk and run and meet people. Dada has no time "for this nonsense" so he designs the shortest distance possible. He needs to learn to relax. He needs to be open to new people. I sense that he is afraid to open up to people he doesn't know. A walk is a walk. People are people. He has yet to learn that. Read on.

You should see how mon père acts when I take him for a walk. Now the world knows that most fox terriers need a lot of exercise, but his majesty doesn't think it applies to me because as you already know, I am not as rambunctious as most of my brothers and sisters. But I do love to walk him. On these walks, he wants to hustle me through the neighborhood as if we were both on fire. He is trying to hurry me on purpose. You should hear him commanding me to poo and pee because he wants to get home to work or eat an early supper or watch a television program. Dogs need to be stimulated to be able to poo specifically. Wonder why such a smart man can't get that through his thick skull?

I like to meet strangers and people who live around the 'hood. My keeper likes to nod and move on. When I see a rabbit or a roadrunner, I want to chase it until I catch it or until it outruns me. Dada instead pulls on my leash like he wants to turn around and go home. He is a big spoilsport.

Now Scott and his dog Riggs are more fun in the great outdoors. Riggs is a good ole' boy, I think partly because of his boxed upbringing. (Can you believe that his sister, also of the box, comes to Full Moon meditations at a lot next door to his house so they get to play once a month? What are the odds even in a small town like Sedona?) Riggs has big ears and his body waddles and shakes when he walks. When we play together daily at the office, Scott takes us outside three times a day to pee and poo. Scott never hurries us or gets mad when we don't do our business. He says to Daddy, "Well, you better take him out a couple of times tonight because he didn't poo."

A few nights back my master gave me a few pieces of delicious chicken without the skin. It was so good that I drank a lot of water. He didn't seem to notice. We went beddy-bye. About 4 o'clock in the morning, I woke after sleeping right next to the snorer and I peed all over him — and me. He jumped out of bed as if we could still get me outside to finish my business. I peed as I ran. He turned on the light on the bedside table and frantically began to shout, "Go, go, run run." As if that would help. He started pulling sheets and padding off the bed. To his credit he did not yell and he did not threaten. Instead, "Mr. Darby, I should have taken you out to pee when I came home from dinner. All this was my fault, not yours."

You could have knocked me over with a feather (another of his favorite expressions). Mister G took responsibility for my actions. To tell the truth, we four-legged creatures do need to be taken outside. As I've said, I haven't figured out how to open the door. At moments like that, il mio papà amazes me.

A goof-ball dog trainer that Dada first consulted told him that he was the Alpha and that I was there to serve him. She brought her "trainer dog" — an ugly fur ball that weighed about three or four pounds wringing wet and was as obnoxious as the Chihuahua in that beer commercial — to show me how to behave. What a nightmare. When she was here in our living room, I wanted to bite her and chase her out the door. But I played along with her nonsense so that mon père would eventually learn that a dog and his owner are in a relationship that requires teamwork, and that living together — even though one of us is a dog — can either be torturous or titillating. I never saw that know-it-all dog trainer again.

Okay, I'll give a timely tip that will always work. It is tantamount to being able to establish peaceful coexistence between a dog and his owner by playing with the dog. I am not talking about throwing a ball in the park for the dog to retrieve for five minutes. It is important to get on the floor or the grass with your dog and show him or her you know how to have a good time. Owners make the mistake of buying silly outfits and parading their pet around Fifth Avenue like it was an Easter Parade. That won't get it. Invest instead in toys and treats or more humane ways to leash and walk your dog. We want affection — true and honest loving intimacy — not elaborate shows like dresses and jackets to make owners feel better about themselves.

DRIVING THE CAR

When I was living on the farm in Iowa, Daryl used to run errands all over the countryside in his truck. At two months old he started taking me on these long hauls. You have probably figured out that I was very inquisitive — what my current keeper calls nosey. I would lay in the seat by Daryl and snooze. One day when I was put in the truck, I hopped in Daryl's lap and I put my paws on the steering wheel. He would shoo me away at first, but after a while I would stay in his lap and drive. Even I know you ain't going to believe that I was actually driving, Dada will tell you that by the time I got to his house and from day one with him, I hopped in his lap and drove away. I will tell off on myself and let you know that this is my defect of character bleeding through. I want to be in charge, even in a car.

There are several reasons why I prefer the driver's seat. Of course, I offer some background. For some unknown and cockamamie notion we four-legs have a lot to teach two-legs. You two-legs seem to have scrambled eggs for brains. You have a pecking order in society like they do in India. A small percentage of you are rich and somewhat famous so you act as though you are better than those less fortunate. Have you ever watched a park full of dogs run and play? Although Dada likes to call attention to my bloodline, I never mention it in the dog park. Believe me, we canines have a lot of conversation amongst ourselves, but we never throw our lineage around. We love to play and act dominant, but it seems we all just play and love to run and chase tennis balls, no matter where we come from. Two-legs could learn a lot about how not to stick their nose in the air and act better than one another.

Another reason I want to drive is because I want to take mon père to places he's never been. In the process, he heard that I wanted to write this book. After a relatively short time together, he became extremely sensitive to me, and he is still learning that where I am taking him is uncharted territory — that it has more to do with what humans have to learn from dogs than how to train, break or make us come into alignment with what smarty pants men and women want us to do. The simple rules of how to get along, pets and parents, are important. It is the other stuff to come that will rock your socks and set you back on your heels.

In the tiny kingdom of Sedona people "Ooh" and "Aah" when they see me with my paws on the steering wheel. I am not a monkey on a stick (a term used for how those fancy ladies in the 1800's in London walked around Piccadilly Square with a monkey on a stick to draw attention to themselves) or a member of a dog and pony show, and I wanted Daddy to know that I did not come all this way from Iowa to be told what to do. What he learned from me is compromise and collaboration. When he sees my paws on the wheel he knows that I am reinforcing what he has learned in spades from me: It takes two to tango for a dog and a human to motor through their lives together.

By the time you read this book I will have turned three years old. Hallelujah! Hallelujah! Hallelujah, Mr. Darby will be all grown up. And for my birthday on October 5th, Daddy has promised to stop saying, "Honey, this is Daddy's baby!" God, how I hate that. Every time he says those repulsive words I yawn. He was so irritated about my constant yawning that he asked Dr. Oler, the vet, why I opened my yapper real wide as if I were bored or disinterested. Dr. Oler asked Daddy why he yawned and Dada said it because he was exhaling. Duh, as Bart Simpson says. I like Dr. Oler. Sometimes I wish he would take me home with him because he says that I am healthy and happy and the best looking dog in Sedona. And he never says, "This is Dr. Oler's baby!" Thank God. What is so annoying most of all with the goo-goo baby talk from Daddy is that he knows that I would rather call him by his real name. He'd rather I call him Prince, which he claims was his nickname growing up. On some deep and connective tissue level he knows that I do not respond to anybody being my daddy or my momma.

GETTING ALONG

Humans have a cross-eyed way of showing love and affection. There seem to be a lot of strings attached: "I will love you if…" "What have you done for me lately…" and it goes on and on. The phrase "I love you" seems to be blackmail on many levels. To get a better handle on relationships, two-legged types should be sentenced to Dog Park duty to see how we in the animal kingdom get along. Sometimes you have a big old bully trying to intimidate me and other small fry. Mon père calls them elephants. But they soon get over their obnoxious selves, we play and tussle, poo and pee and drink water. We love socializing in the dog world and we could show human beings a thing or two about compatibility.

Don't get me wrong. There are some keepers who are more trouble than their dogs. I know one lady who has two weenie dogs and she grabs them when I come near. She says to Daddy, "My dogs do not get along with other dogs," or, "Your Mr. Darby is too aggressive for my angels." One look at her and you know why these dogs need a shrink. They murmur cries all the time they are in the park. Their owner has what Daddy calls a narcissistic grin plastered on her puss. When I first got a gander at her a few months ago, I thought the circus was in town. She is some sideshow that should still be on the inside and not among people or dogs.

But into each life comes sunshine and sheer love, even with humans. When my walker Bob left for ports unknown, it occurred to Daddy that there were a couple of kids around the corner who always give me a treat when we stop to say hello. They are twins, just like Scott and Alison, except these kids are a boy and a girl. The boy twin is real good to me and he has that energy field that says he could be a priest or a saint on Earth. Daddy called and asked the family if one of the kids could walk me every afternoon and they said Thomas could. Bingo! That's the kid! The real surprise was when his twin sister Nikki started to join the Mr. Darby afternoon walk brigade. She is so cute and she loves me to pieces. Nikki always plays with me when she brings me home and I know she likes to be with me. The kids are great, but the one who is over the moon when he sees me coming is their dad, Ed, who runs one of the resort hotel properties. Ed and Dada used to play doubles in tennis until his majesty told too many corny jokes and Ed uninvited Daddy to be his tennis partner.

Despite the end of that relationship, so far, so good with Thomas and Nikki. Because of Nikki's sports activities a kid named Jake comes during the week and I like him a lot. He is so patient and he lets me take as long as I want to do my business. All three of my walkers are only 12, so I hope they last as long as I do. The twins are Italians so Daddy is gaga that he found these two. Thomas is a head shorter than his sister but he has the heart of a mensch and the soul of a saint. He walks slow — which I like — and he takes me to his backyard where we play and I roll around like it's hay in a barn. I always stay an hour, so I have something to look forward to. It amazes me how Daddy and I agree on so many things, particularly Thomas.

Speaking of how humans relate, I am sore as a pimple on an elephant's ass about how these numbskulls dress their dogs like they are trailer trash whores and pimps. If Daddy came near me with a gold collar or walking coat or glitter sh*t on my coat of hair, I would bite him where he keeps the family jewels. Sometimes we go to the pet store and my keeper is either looking for another poo cup to attach to my leash (it's a plastic cup with a plastic tie, and I have a tendency to chew on it when he leaves me in the car — of course with the air conditioning running — so it needs frequent replacing) or a new squeaky toy for Riggs and me to fight over. Just like Mister G has never tried to get me to play "show and tell" or "shine and outshine" other dogs in the park, he doesn't costume me, either. Human beings ought to be ashamed of themselves for spending obscene sums of money on crap for their dogs to wear. Food and water and a good clean, fun home, plus enough exercise is all we want. All of these idiotic shenanigans remind me of that monkey-on-a-stick deal all over again.

Daddy says that I am "nosey Rosie" because he thinks I get into everything. Like when he is sneaking a treat from a box. I can be dead asleep but when I hear the paper crinkle, I race into the kitchen, shake my left paw and plead for even a crumb. Sure, I hear good.

Like the day at the office when I heard Dada tell Linda that I was going to stay with Scott and Alison and Riggs because he is going to New York to visit the Bells and their fox terrier Curtsey. He loves the Bells and he loves Southampton. They will laugh like hyenas for four days and go to the movies and eat scrumptious meals prepared by Chef David. Daddy grovels at David's table like he has never eaten a decent meal in his life. That goes to show you how dumb it was that Daddy never learned to cook. He could have learned from Chef David if he'd just shown interest. But no, my keeper is too disinterested in what it takes to make a good meal, though he's more than happy to eat one.

Thank God il mio papà found fresh food for me and Riggs from Dr. G's Fresh Pet Food. You see, my Mister G met Dr. G's wife at a doctor's office. She was high octane and wearing a twirl skirt. Daddy loves women with a lot of pizzazz and cha-cha-cha on their dance card. I can tell you that I love the food and mon père breaks into shouts of joy over my poo, thanks to Dr. G.

El Beagle, La Madre y Su Hija

I just looked at il mio papà's watch and it is almost time for my first play date with a beagle named Charlie. In case you didn't catch it on Oprah, il principe originally wanted to adopt a beagle like hers. But Dada insisted that it be only a 13-inch beagle, just like Shiloh in the movie of the same name. The owners of Charlie are the couple whose parents own the Red Rock Cafe, which is where Dada eats breakfast every morning at 6:30 a.m., and most lunches with Scott. He saw them at lunch today and asked them to bring their beagle to play in our yard.

Daddy wanted a cute little Shiloh of his own, but his neighbors blew their stack when he told them he was getting a beagle. They threatened and they fumed, daring him to bring a howling yard dog — beagles are known to be more than a bit yippy-yappy — into their classy, quiet, upscale neighborhood.

When Charlie arrived he had his tail between his legs. When my 90-degree up-tail sags, Daddy is always saying, "No, Mr. Darby, this is the Tail of Two Cities — up, up, up." Charlie was small and black all over and Alisha, his mom, explained that they bought him in Tempe from a puppy mill and paid too much but were glad to have him. The minute that blackened sausage sauntered into my yard, Daddy knew that I was going to be overbearing and would scare Charlie with my growl and aggression. Thank God Alisha and Kyle knew the signs of dog play because they coaxed the beagle into chasing me and snapping at me to make me feel as if the play date was going well. It wasn't, and it didn't. I didn't mind Charlie sniffing me a million times but I don't like any dog dude to linger too long around my rear engine.

I hadn't seen Riggs for a couple of days, but I knew I'd see him all day the next day. I guess that Charlie will probably want to hang out with me at least once a week and I guess I will go along with the program, but if I had my druthers I would rather play with Riggs. That Charlie is a piece of work, and he can give as good as he gets. Our friend Windy down the street goes into hyperventilating hysterics when she sees Riggs and me going at it. She's the keeper of that fluff ball Honey Bear who would be eaten alive if Riggs ever got her in his big clapper yapper.

Which brings me to tell you about the two-legged ogre and his mangy looking sheltie I chased the other day, with Daddy hollering for me to come back. The sheltie's keeper, an old c*ck*ucker, kept muttering about people who let their wild dogs off tether while mon père panted and shuffled after us. Daddy hollered to the ogre, "Please stop so I can get my dog." The old grouch growled back, "I will not. This damn dog is your responsibility. Come and get him or leave him to the wild drivers. They'll take care of him."

My keeper finally reached this man and his dog and me. The bearded discontent was not through railing at Daddy and me. "Keep this mutt chained or tethered. You are an irresponsible asshole." It was then Mister G's turn. "And you, sir, are reprehensible and not a good neighbor. I will thank you to keep your uncivil comments to yourself." I had a giddy-up in my prance back to our overpriced adobe and had great pride in my keeper. That old fool gives dog owners a bad name. Imagine the hell-hole the sheltie skulks around in. Poor chap.

Now I've got to weigh in on these two Mexicans, mother and daughter, who clean our house on Saturdays. La madre speaks English as does la hija — and I know very little Spanish except what Daddy translates for me from an online Spanish-to-English web site. But because I am writing about Spanish-speaking ladies, I wanted to give a little Español here and there. The best part of them is que aman los perros. (They love dogs. Arf! Arf!) Lucky for me and better for them as I can act out and act up worse than that bozo Ashton Kutcher when I am ignored or treated badly. But they come in and give me all the amor that Mexico allows.

Last Saturday the best thing la madre Dora did was to get all the poo out of Daddy's new million-thread count Egyptian cotton duvet. Her exact words were, "No hay problema." I thought he was going to besarle los pies. Figure that one out for yourselves.

One of the things that I am ga-ga over about Daddy is how open-minded he is. A few weeks ago la madre Dora told Daddy that she could not afford to drive thirty miles each way on the money he was paying her. "Asi que lo siento pero debo dar mi renuncia," she said. What she really wanted to say was, "I ain't working for slave wages. I can get a lot more from other houses I clean, you cheapskate." The clean version translation? "I do not feel I can continue to work for you so I am giving notice." Mon père hastened to tell her, "No hay problema." He then gave her a raise in pay so she was grateful and decided to stay.

Which brings me to the issue of the law that the half-cracked governor Jan Brewer of the State of Arizona crammed down the throats of its citizens: Bill 1080, or the Arizona Immigration Law. Bottom line, this bill discriminates against Mexicans and all other foreigners, specifically through intimidation and perhaps through unlawful detainment and incarceration. All the big Ike movie stars and liberals (another way of saying people who care about all people, not just the rich and entitled) are slamming the state. Add my bow-wow to those who disapprove. Daddy told me that our ladies from South of the Border are here lawfully and are not afraid of that law, but no Spanish-speaking people like the bill. One day I will write about Sheriff Joe Arpaio, the loco lawman in Phoenix, Arizona who makes jailbirds wear pink jumpsuits as a way to deter them from breaking the law. What a nut job he is. Los autoridades federales just served him papers for making his own rules of incivility and trying to enforce his own brand of justice with illegal shenanigans. These dirty tricks could get him a long stretch in his haute pink tent prison. Thank God Dada is law-abiding. He's cash register-honest, and he tells the truth to each and every one because he would commit Hari-Kari if he had to spend five minutes in the hoosegow.

NIKKI, THE BEST TWO-LEGGED LITTLE GIRL IN MY LIFE

So much for Daddy bringing me to Sedona so he could get more exercise. Man, can Dada lie to himself, big time. He is at long last dropping the weight as if it were his life's ambition, but it's not because he's walking me more. It seems that his accountant Mark lost 80 pounds in four months by eating a new food regimen out of ooh-la-la Paree, Ideal Protein. So my keeper skedaddled over to sign up for the same eating plan with Maryanne, the doyenne of diet loss, who herself dropped 40 pounds as if it were a few ounces. Dada's lost more than 30 pounds in six months and does he ever look a few years younger. However, because the food is pre-packaged and all protein, his heart doctor put the skids on it and he is now scarfing down oatmeal every morning and has a snack at night.

Pause. This entry is not about Dada, but about Nikki, one of the twins who walk me every day at 4 in the afternoon.

Nikki is fun to be with because she understands that a dog needs to let 'er rip when he is in the Dog Park or sniffing around on the golf course or rooting around in a dirt pile in her backyard. Her dad was allergic to dogs, and then he learned I am a non-allergy animal. From then on he would play pitch and fetch with me. I stayed with the family for five days once when mon père was in New York on business. I hated to come home because I felt like royalty in the Zielinski household.

Here is the lowdown on Nikki, all twelve years old of her. She is sweet and patient, neither of which describes Daddy. She chases me and then I run after her. If I splash in a puddle she always laughs and says, "Daddy's gonna get on us. He hates for you to come home wringing wet." And I mind-to-mind tell her, "Not if he can't catch us," and we both tumble down the embankment and get wetter and dirtier. When we come storming home soaked to the skin in dirty water, Dada makes a noise as if we had robbed a bank or bitch-slapped him. And all we were doing is what comes naturally to a twelve-year-old girl and a two-year-old dog with peerage who knows how to play the game "two-leggeds versus four-leggeds."

The minute we get back from my daily constitutional (Google the term and you will know what it means if you haven't caught on yet), my keeper always wants to know, "Did Mr. Darby potty?" If she says that I did, Daddy is over the moon with joy. "My precious angel went to the bathroom!"

If she says that I didn't, he growls and yanks my leash and turns me out into the backyard and he hollers as I flee, "Go potty, Mr. Darby and I mean it." Then he mumbles that he won't feed me another t-r-e-a-t and he might get my old crate out of storage. Bah, humbug. They're all idle threats. I act like I did No. 2 (that is a puritanical Southerner's way of talking about sh*t) and I wag my tail and wait for my treat that tastes just like peanut butter. In five minutes I am curled up on my side of the bed, feigning sleep, so the two-legged one will stop talking goo-goo baby talk to me.

He blogs all the time about everything from the revolution in Egypt to prayers for Charlie Sheen, who as I said before is one of the goofiest and dumbest bells I have ever heard ring among two-leggeds. Egypt's have-nots won the battles and the war, but Charlie may be looking at life in prison — self-imposed.

As I write this the value of our casa in Sedona continues to fall through the floor, our bank accounts are shrinking and our grass in the backyard died during the winter. But the one thing that is alive and well here in Red Rock Valhalla in my little corner of the world is that I eat as much as a 20-pounder needs, my water bowl has clean, clear water with breath-fresh droplets and I get to run and play with all the mongrels, curs, rescues and peerage four legs of all ages, weight and lengths. Sometimes I get treats. Humans may be waiting for death and destruction in 2012 (it's getting harder and harder to lift the spirits of greedy, selfish, "it's all about me" Homines sapientes), but they'll get what they get by doing what they do.

9

CHALLENGES FOR MY KEEPER

Sometimes I think I am on top of things. Like the other night when Daddy called Starr, the Dog Whisperer, who turned my relationship with Daddy around for the better when I was six months old. He told Starr about how much he had grown considering my recent poo accidents. Dada poured it on real thick. He has Leo ascending in his birth chart — and so do I — so you would have thought he was on stage getting applause and a paycheck. I didn't mind because he said he never had kids or a puppy before, and it was he who had to accept a potty accident and not me who was to blame and ought to be punished. She told him she missed me. I have stayed with her and her husband when Daddy has gone out of town, and like I do with mon père, I slept with her and her husband.

Now for the big news. Daddy has been going through some rough patches, or as his Granny used to say, "Baptism by fire." It seems that there has been a big hullabaloo over the crumbling economic picture here and across all oceans, and it has stirred up mon père real bad. As a matter of fact he talked to one of those "big pieces of stuff" business tycoons who told Daddy that the time had come for Scott to find another job. Dada's company could not support two salaries under the economic dark clouds. I have never seen il mio papà so downtrodden and unhappy. Every time he heard "The world as it was for you and Scott as business partners is over," he bawled like a baby. "The train has left the station. It's finished," said the man resolutely.

When Dada came to bed he tossed and turned. He talked in his sleep. At first I thought he had tee-teed on the sheets because he likes to hug me tight, like I am his life raft or something or other, but it turned out to be sweat. I know he has vivid dreams which are like movies because he yaks all night. If I were a steno I could write them down and sell them on the black market. Anyhow he had a restless night in Sedona.

The next morning after breakfast he was working on the computer. Again, for someone who thinks the computer is the anti-Christ, he spends a lot of time writing on the damn thing. All of a sudden I heard this bawling, sobbing, heartbreaking cry coming from his work space. I perked up to listen to make sure he was the one under emotional duress. It was my keeper, for sure. After a few minutes, I went tearing into the computer room and I jumped in his lap to console him. It made him cry even more. But he understood that I was coming to the rescue. He and I have developed an innate symbiosis that would surprise a lot of dog owners who don't have a clue what exactly we dogs are doing in their lives. Daddy gets it in spades. I know my care and concern for him made him feel a lot better.

Scott arrived a few minutes after this emotional meltdown, Riggs in tow, so naturally I sped to the backyard where the 60-pounder and I could give Scott and Daddy a real canine show. Riggs and I snarl and growl — we chase and I grab him around the neck with my teeth. He grabs my harness and slings me back and forth. When we first started this dog play months ago, both of these grown men thought we were wolves trying to decide which was the Alpha in the pack. Now they love to watch us have at it.

The minute Daddy started to talk to Scott again, he began to cry. The tears were caused by the pain mon père felt about what his friend had said to him about business, and him and Scott and budgets. All Dada could think about was the impending birth of Scott's and Alison's twin daughters. Scott admitted that there was no way he and Dada could continue as they were; that it was time for him to strike out on his own and make a life for him and his family that was not dependent on Daddy and the company. Scott and Daddy have worked together for more than fourteen years. It seemed as if the ceiling had caved in on Daddy and Scott.

"My friend," Scott said, "I know you never want to admit it but you are getting up in years even though you think you'll work until you die at 102, but I need to start a career on my own, putting down roots in a job that I can work for many years to come. It is time we faced reality." He hugged Daddy and they both shed a few tears.

Scott is a smart cookie. He was empathetic to Daddy's character and said that "they broke the mold when they made him." He was trying to help Dada face reality about the conditions in which all of us are operating. Scott wanted to guide Daddy to be more stable financially. Thank the good Lord that il principe was able to adjust his moolah so I could stay put and continue to eat two square dog meals a day.

"I will stay as financial officer from a distance as long as it works for you. You do not like anything to do with the IRS or balancing the checkbook. This I can do and still work at Big Brothers Big Sisters."

Dada smiled and said that he would like that. And he told Scott that he would come to see him and Alison and the twins on weekends. And this he has done as religiously as a Baptist going to church on Sunday.

Riggs and Scott and I left for the office. As I've mentioned, every day when I come home from the office Daddy always asks me if "I brought home the bacon." That is another one of those corny Southern expressions that I loathe. He is always threatening to move back to Alabama and I mutter, "Over my dead body!" Anyway, Riggs and I love to be together and we are like two brothers, but we are definitely from a different litter. I am older but Riggs is a lot bigger so he likes to dominate. I let him but only after a lot of tug-and-war.

When mon père came to the office, he had talked with his close friend Harriet. I understand she is little and feisty and speaks her mind every chance she gets. He says that if Harriet ran the world we would all be happier, like the Seven Dwarfs, whistling as we work. Loving whomever we wanted to — gay, straight or in between and taking the credit and discredit for what we did or didn't do.

Harriet agreed with Daddy's business associate. She said that Daddy and his secretary should write up a new menu of services, activate this new-fangled internet phenomenon called Skype which would allow him to work with clients online rather than travel all the time. Harriet said that Scott should continue to handle the finances. "He knows how to keep your feet to the fire. Changing the way you spend money is going to take someone like Scott who can rein you in when you go overboard financially, " she said to Daddy. She went on to tell him that nobody in the world can do what he does — that he shoots from the lip and lets the chips fall where they may.

What a stand-up, true blue friend this broad is. I want to meet her. But Daddy says she has a sausage dog so she might have to come north to meet me in my own backyard.

Mon père must have had one of those "shifts" he's always crowing about. He was calm as a cucumber talking to Harriet. When we went to bed, he let me go to my own bed early and did not pick me up and he didn't even put me in his bed when he got up in the middle of the night to go to the bathroom. He always tells the clients under emotional siege, "This, too, shall pass," and his emotional meltdown gave way to calmer, clearer, waters. I may poke fun at him from time to time, but he never ceases to amaze me. This dude walks his talk.

I have noticed that he keeps problems and solutions up-close and personal. When his clients ask about the state of the union or conditions of unrest all over the world, he advises them: "Change you to change the world." Sounds smart to me. I love it when he tells a mean and bitchy gut-eater, "Become the change you want to see in the world." My favorite is, "Get out of the blame game."

Remember that I sit beneath the feet of his dented and dinged clients doing the spiritual healing, like the Hopi Grand Poo-Bah says, "from the feet up." Dada doesn't predict, he indicates. He never prophesizes but rather he points out trends that might lead to rack and ruin unless the man or woman changes how they live and feel and think.

My favorite avoidance of his is refusing to be a wild-haired seer in a flowing white robe sprinkling star dust as he walks. Lately, when he lectures, someone in the audience always asks him what is going to happen in December 2012, the supposed end of the Mayan Calendar. He always answers, "Nothing. Next question?" He was living in Sedona during the Harmonic Convergence in August 1987 and when he was asked what was going to happen, he said, "Nothing." And nothing did happen except a gaggle of fools paid some con man thousands of dollars for first class seats on the first UFO that landed and took off for the wild blue yonder. I learned fast about these woo-woo fairy dusters in Sedona.

What a guy. My observation is that people who get into the spiritual woo-woo business have always got to be promoting something spectacular or dazzling. Daddy helps change lives one person at a time, and that is the bottom line reason I got him to pick up the phone and talk to my former mother Millie about buying me and coming to live with him in Sedona.

Chew on that. Whatever you do in the meantime, be good to you.

DON'T LET THE BED BUGS BITE

It's il principe ranting and raving at the computer again, calling the internet the Anti-Christ—again. He says that any dodo with a computer and a third grade education can let loose with nonsense all over the world with the click of a SEND button. Sometimes the news is not as dumbed-down as it is disgusting. Read on.

He was reading to me the other night about a global epidemic with bed bugs in hotels, retirement homes, hospitals and other places frequented by the 'n- and-out crowd, touristas! He was referencing those teeny tiny nasty blood sucking vermin that hide in mattresses and in headboards and other convenient secret nooks that never seem to be cleaned properly.

Just when I thought we were done with the subject, His Grace's super pal Gail calls from New York to report that her mother's retirement home had been attacked by an army of bed bugs and that the attendants have been throwing all the patient's clothing into the communal washing machine to sanitize them. This included her mother's designer skirt and sweater which p*ssed Gail off big-time. They were boiling bedding in scalding hot water and combing mattresses with a fine tooth comb to make sure that not one of these nasty, stinking, filthy icky creepy crawlers would still be alive when they finished fumigating every nook and cranny in that home for the precious gifted souls over 90. Gail said that the whole place was topsy-turvy. When Daddy saw her mother in that facility in April, he said she looked 60 (just turned 95) and was as happy as a doting dowager having tea at three — or something like that. Since that episode Nan has flown away to the Other Side of Life which I call The Perfect Place. Daddy loved Nan because they had the same silly sense of humor. Brother did she have 5,280 opinions about everything, just like you-know-who.

While we are on the subject of lowlife in Americana, let's talk about the trailer trash vermin and riffraff like the Lindsay Lohans, Paris Hiltons, and some degenerates known as Jersey Shore, drinking and drugging and acting like the world is waiting to see or smell them. Every time someone in the neighborhood knocks on our door and asks this household to send tax-free dole out to the local schools, Daddy always says that he and Mr. Darby will give our fair share when the kids pull their pants up, girls stop dressing like pole-dancing hookers and scholastic achievement is raised to heights that show education is really teaching our kids what they are there to learn and keeping them out of jails and rehab centers.

THE KNEE TAILS, ERR, TALES

Life is full of surprises, but none bloodier than the sight I saw when I returned from a recent afternoon walk. Daddy was in the bed with his left leg on a pile of pillows and he was telling Scott on his cell phone that his knee started to swell while he was eating his supper on a TV tray in front of the tellie, as the Brits call the "boob tube," while he was watching Joy Behar. Joy's guest was Rachel Ray, a knock-out honey who cooks on the tellie for a living. I was smacking my lips watching my new favorite sexpot while licking Daddy's left knee.

Soon Scott arrived to examine the damage and I went out of my gourd jumping and loving on him. Scott is really the best of all the rest. He may be stricter than mon père, but he also has the time to make over me and I am in ecstatic euphoria with him.

He brought ice bags and a pee-pot to his bed since Daddy said it was too painful to walk ten steps to the commode. Scott piled the pillows sky-high and plopped ice bags on top and on the side of il principe's knee. In a matter of minutes, Daddy decided that he wanted to go to ER to have the knee drained. He was due to leave for New York in a few days to officiate at the wedding of one of his Broadway actor friends.

So off they went to see the quacks at the hospital. I know what happened because Daddy loves to give me a blow-by-blow account when anything catastrophic happens to him. (Any psycho-babble bloviator would refer to this as "pillow talk" — that's when he blabs a lot about the spiritual life in Sedona or his aching back or knee).

They got to the ER and there were no sick and dying patients in the waiting room — just Daddy and his favorite ER medic, Dr. Dean. Evidently, because Dada was not screaming as if he were dying, the doc went straight to the knee with a needle as long as his arm (though I'm sure this is another of Daddy's exaggerations), rammed it into his left knee and drained a lot of fluid and blood. Daddy's blood pressure was reasonable and the doc told him that he was in a better state of mind and not as loud and disruptive as when he was in the ER in April. That's when Daddy lambasted a little old Pink Lady volunteer who was directing traffic and taking names who tried to get him to shut up. "You're disturbing the other patients, sir. If you don't hush I'll have to ask you to leave." And with that threat he hobbled and chased this weathered and trusted hospital servant around screaming, "I'll show you, you crazy, nutty lady from Malaysia." And with that threat his name was called, he was wheeled into a holding station where his knee was emptied of all the gunk and bloody fluid. He came home and slept like a baby with all the morphine the doctor allowed.

This time was a different story. Pink Lady was not on duty, rather a beehive hairdo high school dropout named Joyce checked him right in, and Dr. Dean did his number. Dada and Scott came home within an hour. Thank God that Daddy's intuition was on high alert because he vibed the perfect time to have his knee seen.

When Dada picked me up and put me in his bed, I stayed put against my better judgment. It was because he whispered as he fell asleep, "Now for the real therapy from the accidental healer, Mr. Darby." And so while he went to visit Mr. Sandman, I snuck under the covers and went to work on that bum knee.

The next day, it rained early in the morning and Dada got his tightie whities in a wad when I was unable to potty in the Dog Park. Scott has told him a zillion times that rain washes away the smells we dogs like in order to do our business. But what Daddy did instead was to let me out in the backyard twice in a couple of hours, and I handled what I needed to do for myself.

Mister G went off to see this new orthopedic doctor he is crazy about, Dr. Brad Williams, who is young and apparently engaging. Anyway, he got in to see Dr. Brad when he called, and he had an audience scheduled with the good doctor at 8:30 a.m. Scott came for me so Riggs and I spent the day with him. Linda was out with her son's leg problem, and the plan was for me to stay four nights with Riggs. Oh, that homophobic Marine looked in the window and of course Riggs and I were all over one another's mouths and the Marine screamed, "Homos, homos!" No one could tell, but Riggs and I got a huge charge from this silly savage.

Daddy came by the office to report that the doctor drained more fluid from his left knee and injected him with a steroid shot. Dr. Brad has now decided that he will try an arthroscopic procedure to clean up the knee, which made Daddy deliriously happy. He knows too many people with knee replacements who are still suffering months afterwards.

As Dada walked out of the office, I went to the see-through door and watched him as he left. The truth be told, he and I are more of a perfect fit than I make out sometimes. It is just that he goes so overboard trying to please me and love me and wanting to be reassured. He's got to get it through his noggin that if I had known we were misfits I would have skedaddled back to Iowa as fast as the airlines could take me. But he's a keeper. Man, when he reads this he will be in some kind of ecstasy. Apparently he's not the only one who can't keep his yapper shut.

BURY ME AT WOUNDED KNEE

When my aging and not so agile Dada came home from high-jinks New York late on a Sunday night, he had a lot to say about his quick turnaround trip. Just when he thought he had turned the corner with his tricky swollen left knee, his friend David had to take him to the Southampton ER at midnight his first night on Long Island. Blood on the knee, again! Mon père made quite a racket in the ER to such a decibel levels that the admission's witch must have been sister to the one at the Sedona Medical Center ER because she told him to pipe down. "Shut up that wailing if you want to be admitted." Apparently, Daddy was too exhausted and in too much pain to run her off because he hushed and waited for the doc to drain the knee. Daddy told Scott that he had to have an almost lethal dose of narcotics before the pain subsided.

Now I will weigh in as an emotional and medical analyst who did not go to Harvard Medical School or any other crackpot institution of medicine. Every time he has to fly, Daddy has a knee-jerk reaction, no pun intended. It used to be a kidney stone attack, ER and all, and then emotional overload settled in his left knee. For days before he has to get on an airplane — he says that even First Class is like riding in a smelly old bus — he tells anybody who will listen how much he does not look forward to five hours on any airline.

My prognosis is that he has been under a lot of stress for a long time. Not being married or in a committed relationship (it makes me want to throw up to suggest that a relationship could be his remedy), he absorbs all the hurt, guilt, pain, negativity, shame and blame and a million other toxic forms of character defects that are dumped on him by his clients. It is a lot like the stigmata. He seems to need to suffer what others can't bear. So, ladies and gentlemen of the jury, Mr. Lord and Master of Souls of the Universe is having his body break down because he is in overload. He is almost kaput and in an altered state of needing major overhaul and release to let go of what others bring to him. Don't think I have not been telling him every night before he turns out the light. And the only upside to all this nonsense is that he and I are getting closer and closer. He never yells or threatens or manhandles me. He kisses me like I am a Venus de Milo with four paws.

THROUGH THE LOOKING GLASS

Ladies and gentlemen of the jury, for your information, this world is not the real world. The earth is "here" and where we come from and return to "there." "Here" is a reform school for bad boys and bad girls—and dogs and cats and all other animals—to redeem ourselves. I know we live in an energetic universe — that we all, including animals, are all-seeing and all-knowing. So is it any wonder that I finagled my way into Dada's life?

We all live in parallel planets. When things get too tough to handle, we go into a secret hiding place that protects us from knowing the whole truth and nothing but the truth. To insulate ourselves from disappointment in love or to avoid responsibilities that require scrubbing dirty floors, we sidle into the dimly-lit theatre of the mind. Life for all of us is about service to others.

Do you want to know why I chose to be of service to my Daddy? Do you want to know why I liked him from the minute I picked up on him through cosmic radar? He and I are both a bit strange. Mon père and I are odd ducks if the truth be told. From my observations at floor level, those of us who are more uniquely assembled have a greater chance of listening to the Divine when He/She/It speaks to us. Those who seek the headiness of klieg lights and fame cannot seem to find the compass to their inner sanctum—the soul room.

I'm not a lot like my breed and he sure as shootin' is not a lot like his tribe. And if he has made a commitment to endorse our truth and only the truth, he is going to tell you that I taught him a lot — and that is the gospel, as they say in the South where he was born. But he who teaches learns, as Dada is wont to say from time to time, so I must declare that he taught me a heck of a lot as well.

Since no one can really crucify me for being bold and more direct than he has ever been (After all, what does a dumb dog know? Right? Wrong!), I think the humility it took for him to let me write this book is amazing. You can tell from how I express myself through him that he has let me reveal a lot about him, a lot more than most men of his statue would have, and I am not talking about his height. I am speaking of all the lives he has affected yet he makes so little of it. He is letting me call him out because at his age he wants to be at peace with himself. Letting me write as I do allows him to love himself. He likes to tell clients and audiences that he is closer to the Exit door than most people he knows. (He's talking After Life here, for those newcomers to Consciousness.) You humans are real weird. You always want to purge your souls — to be up close and personal — when what you really need is to have more fun.

10

THINGS THEY ARE A CHANGIN'

Once Dada and Scott took me to New York to meet Daddy's publishers. On the flight, I was in a carry-on doggie bag with a mesh front so I could breathe. Remembering my inaugural flight to Sedona I tried to claw open the lining to free myself. Scott knew I was panicking so he tore the mesh open so I could stick my head out. He petted me to make me less anxious.

The old hag flight attendant shook her finger at me and said to mon père, "If that mutt gets out of that bag, you're going to be in a lot of trouble." And Daddy said, "You touch my dog and you're going to wish you were scrubbing floors in the poorhouse in Mississippi."

But I digress. I have been on a tear to have a bitch in the house. She can sleep with me and although we won't be able to have kids, we can adopt. Can't you see it now? Mon père, who never had a kid or even an animal in his life until I arrived, letting me and my lady adopt a couple of poopers? That'd be the day. But I still want a lady friend in my life.

Daddy will say we can't afford another mouth to feed. He'd be channeling his mother Marguerite who used that as excuse to her brood for never having a pet while they were growing up. I know that the economy is screwed up all over the world but we could let go of the housekeeper or cut her hours back — eat in more and save almighty dollars — just so we could add a prissy frilly bitch under our adobe flat roof casa.

What pisses me off is that two-leggeds always think the president or a senator or a congressman got them into financial trouble. These bozos got themselves into this deep despair of not enough money to go around. Daddy grew up in an era when if a kid wanted to go to the movies or have a bicycle, he cut lawns or did other chores. Mon père blogs and preaches that the credit card system and the internet are Siamese twins of mass destruction. He thinks that when someone has a yen for something in today's world and can't afford it, they either charge it or steal it. Or when someone has something to say, whether or not they have been classified and certified as nuts or loony tunes, they can spew it all over the internet. If you want to know the level of insanity in the world today, read all those Blogs that have polarized the world of two-legs like there will be no tomorrow. If this hatred doesn't stop there won't be a tomorrow or a day after tomorrow.

We can't leave the issue of the Blame Game alone. When the Great Unwashed get through slimming the president and Congress, they blame the Jews or the Blacks for what's wrong in the world. Daddy tells everyone that 2012 is about nothing, but what he really thinks is that if all the kooks and crackpots in this country don't start taking responsibility for the sorry state of affairs they helped create, a big black fire and brimstone hole will open up and swallow the snivelers and blamers and generally degenerate sector of the masses. He further says that they better hope that if indeed there is no heaven with streets paved with gold that Saint Paul better be on hand to give each blamer a hoe and a sack of seed to grow what they eat.

Il mio papà is a pisser himself, but in a good way. Mr. "It's all about all of us" Dada has come full circle — from a "charge it" thousandaire living years ahead on plastic, to an "if I ain't got it I don't spend it" financially-conscious human being. He started out as a young boy very aware that if he wanted something he better pay for it. The only way to get something in the 40's and 50's was to put it on layaway, and when the pants or pocketbook was paid for, you took it from the department store. Today, mon père uses a debit card from his bank. He no longer has revolving credit. Praise God from whom all blessings flow.

Now that I'm a house regular, Dada comes to my perch atop 1,000-count Pratesi sheets on his million-dollar bed like one the King and Queen of England sleep on, just to give me kisses. What a difference a year makes. He used to slap my behind when I did not poo on his schedule or pee in the yard at dawn when he got up. Daddy would turn red in the face and holler at the top of his lungs when I didn't eat when he said so. Scott helped a lot when he said, "Let Mr. Darby eat when he's hungry." Scott may not be a genius but he is a dog's best friend, as is his wife Alison. I can't wait to give their babies a welcome lick into this world. Man, are those twins lucky to have Scott and Alison as parents and Riggs as a brother. I think I will be included in their inner circle as Daddy is going to claim Grand Poobah when the babies move onto Jordan Road. For those of you writing doctoral dissertations on my book, you need to know that Grand Poobah was a name given to a self-important person in Gilbert & Sullivan's opera, The Mikado. I rest my case.

THE TWINS

On October 22, 2010, Livia and Augusta came bounding onto the Planet Earth and you would have thought they belonged to il mio papà. He went speeding up Oak Creek Canyon to Flagstaff to get a first glimpse of these special bundles of joy. He brought Alison a 10-pound tome from that Oprah favorite, Ken Follett — as if she would have time to read. (Five months later all Alison has time for is breastfeeding and walking and rocking the look-alikes.) The doctor says they are identical, but I'll bet my last sou they will never ever be dressed alike.

When I got my first gander at these two beautiful chillun, all I wanted to do was sniff them out. After all, I am a Wire Fox Terrier. Daddy got the great idea to send out a Diaper Account Announcement to solicit financial help from all their family and friends with the cost of diapering two infants. Scott inserted a USA Today newspaper article that said it would cost $40 a week per child. Although math is not my strong suit, I can figure that those diapers are going to cost a hell of a lot of moolah.

The two cutie patooties are wailers and squallers. Scott comes into the office every day looking like a zombie, or like a father who has been up and down all night with his baby girls. Some days, Alison can barely move with the demands of nursing and nurturing her new arrivals.

Dada is amusing to watch when he is holding one of them. He talks to them like they are grown-ups — no baby talk from him — and he tells them he is il principe and when they are older they can kiss his sterilized 18-carat gold Egyptian ring.

My brother from another litter, Riggs, is more territorial than his parents. He usually greets with a lot of kisses and dog play, but when I tear through his house he growls like the ferocious red heeler he is and he dares me to come near his sisters. Scott has to calm him down and he lets me smell the babies in their blankets. I get so excited that I sometimes wet myself and their new wooden floors. If Daddy is holding one of them and Livia or Augusta start crying, mon père hands the baby off as fast as God would have it. He definitely did not sign on to rock these girls to sleep, or at least not until they stopped crying.

My keeper has known Scott for fourteen years now, and Scott was a bachelor for most of those years. He and Daddy traveled all over the world, cavorting in Italy and Spain, Egypt, South America and in major cities in his country to see clients and most of all to rediscover people, places and things they had known before. Remember, Daddy and Scott and I all believe in reincarnation so that's why I refer to them as rediscovering these sites.

The year before Scott married, Daddy did his annual update on Scott's astrological birth chart. My keeper told him that he and Alison were going to have twins. He was shocked and didn't really pay much attention to the wizard and his prediction. And when the baby doctor told them that they were having twins, Alison was floored, but Scott at least was not too wowed.

Having twins has certainly been a challenge for the two of them, but Scott's mother Carol has helped so Alison and Scott could get some sleep. His Dad Barry and step-mother Peggy have traveled all the way from Ohio to rock crying babies and change diapers. Alison's mother Margie has been the saint. She practically lived with Scott and Alison the first six months the babies were born. Now she comes on Wednesdays. Dada has tried to get her named Grandmother of the Year in Arizona.

What amazes me is how all their friends and family have given them so many pieces of equipment. You sure need a lot for babies. (It sure as hell is cheaper for us four-legs to have litters. When we are weaned, we are off and running to the next adventure: adoption.) The babies got swings and baby carriages and bassinets and car seats, plus clothes that are fit for real princesses. Some friend named Gottsch gave them a princess "time-out" chair and tons of clothes and shoes. When Daddy was in Paris for the French Open in 2010, he bought them Le Petit Bateau outfits. He has a picture of them in one little frock as his screensaver on his computer.

GOOD-BYE, MR. RIGGS

Mon père has a few friends in Sedona and elsewhere in the last few months whose dogs have died or have had to be put to sleep. He tells me how much these keepers miss their lifelong best friends and how hard it is for them get a new dog. It sure as hell is not like trading in a dying car for a brand new one. And it's not just humans who grieve the loss of a pet. We are sad when we lose our best friends, too.

Just today his friend Chip who is a plumber stopped by our car to pet me. (Chip fixed one of our toilets and Dada swore for an hour when he saw the bill. He calmed down when his new assistant Danni told him that Geter Plumbing was the most knowledgeable in town and worth every penny when you consider what they have to do.) Dada told me that Chip's 10 years old Maltese named Annie had to be put to sleep last year because she had cancer. If she was anything like Chip I would have liked to have known her. He said he liked my Nancy Reagan red sweater that I intuited mon père to get me for Christmas. This is not the same as human need to "dress-up" their dog. It gets cold out here and when the temperature drops to 18 degrees you beat your arse a Wire Fox Terrier shivers and shakes from the cold.

I lost my best friend Riggs less than a year ago, but it's not because he left this Earth. He just left my immediate area. Scott and Alison felt that having twins and a dog was too much to deal with. Scott is very stoic, but also very practical, according to Dada. He felt he had to find Riggs new parents and lots of land where he could be the Australian Shepherd Red Healer mix that he is. When Scott's horse Magic had to be put down a few years ago because of colic, Scott held Magic's head while he went to sleep. He drove home and cried privately and then went on with his life.

Scott found Riggs a big ranch thirty miles from Sedona where he could live with a couple who took to Riggs from the minute he came to their house.

I love the way adults make decisions for us dogs. If they'd asked me, I would have asked if Riggs could live with me and mon père rather than let him go away so I would never see him again. Daddy said when he was young and the family moved from one state to another they had to leave playmates behind. Makes sense to two-leggeds, but not to us four paws on the floor. I was so torn up about Riggs going away that I still went to the backyard door every day just like I always did, waiting and wanting to play with him. My high and mighty keeper kept telling me that Riggs wouldn't be coming back. I'll never forget the day I got the news about Riggs. Dada opened the door and I went outside. I laid down in the grass behind the hedge and wept. There will never be another Riggs for me, ever. He and I bonded and breathed each other's breath and we loved to try to out-Alpha the other. I know one day I will see him Over There where we go when we kick the bucket.

What really pisses me off is that Riggs and I never got to have that last chase over the wall to drop a big load behind the bushes next to the golf course. I am five months older than Riggs and when he was only seven weeks old, I was the dominant one. Today he is 60-plus pounds and I weigh less than two stone. Wanna know who is the alpha dog in my own yard? The one who got away, and I miss the dominance like crazy. Daddy called his friend Kid Bell and told him that I was blue and moping around. I was actually considering running after Riggs to see if the rancher and his old lady would take me in. I understand that Riggs is going to work for his biscuits herding horses. Rumor has it that he may have to live outdoors, and that's where I would draw the line. I plop my butt atop Pretesi sheets and sleep with a down comforter. Scott called Riggs' new family and the mother said that Riggs was in door every night. Jeez, my prayer has been answered.

What I despise about two-leggeds is that when someone dies, they weep and wail and then a day later, they act as if nothing ever happened. It is a known fact that we canines grieve for two months before we are able to get over the death of another dog. But the bottom line of why we feel the loss of a pal like Riggs so deeply is because we bond through the simple things we do. It is because we four-legged creatures like running free in the woods or smacking our lips at the mention of a treat or splashing in the creek in red rock country. Trouble-free things like a play date or when Dada makes a fuss over a good potty — that makes my day. Or when Daddy wakes me up and scratches my back and massages the top of my head. I guess that two-legs are always looking for something to make them feel better, usually only things that money can buy. Riggs made my day and finished it off when he went home. I will miss him as long as I live.

THE LORD TAKETH AWAY, THEN AN UNEXPECTED GIVETH

When Dada eats at the Red Rock Cafe breakfast and lunch every day, I sit in the Mercedes with air conditioning in the summer and heat in the winter. He cracks the window so I can meet and greet all the diners. Sometimes friskier dogs howl and bay at the non-existent moon for hours while I curl up on mon pere's warm driver's seat and nap. (After we turn three, we Wire Fox Terriers only know two speeds: full ahead and sleep).

Two ladies have come to my car window practically every day at the cafe and coo and make over me, and of course I eat it up every time. They bring treats — treats that I would murder to get. Dada was told by the vet that I was a few stones too heavy so he rations my food like I am a two-ton Tubby.

Anyway, it seems that these ladies interrogated my keeper until he gave them the name of my breeders, Millie and Daryl. Wouldn't you know, they followed through and bought a puppy from my former parents in Bloom-field, Iowa.

This little ball of fire full of piss and vinegar arrived a few weeks ago, and il principe and I went over to their house to meet him. He was 10 pounds at 10 weeks old, and his name is Jesse. Dada made over him like he was a prince-in-waiting — just like he did when I arrived at la casa three years ago. Funny thing is that Jesse is my half-brother, same mother, different daddy.

Well, Dada carried on over Jesse like I didn't exist. Of course, Jesse ate it up. Jesse jumped in mon père's lap and nipped at his fingers. He charmed Daddy out of his senses.

The odd thing is that Jesse, according to my lord and master, looks just like I did at that age. He came to our house and we played in the yard. I let Jesse know that he is the much younger bro, and I am the dominant one in this neighborhood. Dada made arrangements for him and me to have weekly play dates.

I have been tuning in mind-to-mind with my Dada lately not to tell anyone else in Sedona where Jesse and I came from. Before you know it he and I would be referred to as the four-legged version of the Beverly Hillbillies. God forbid.

To tell the truth I kind of like having Jesse around, especially because I miss Riggs. Jesse's not just someone to boss around the yard, but another four-legged creature to play with and love.

If humans think we dogs don't have feelings when our playmates die or move away, they are sadly mistaken. Loss for a dog is just as hard on us as it is for humans. Dada sees me shed tears and thank the Lord he knows when I am feeling low. He was so sensitive when I lost my friend Riggs that he and I had a good cry together. For some reason, I think I will see Riggs again. But then, again, as Dada likes to say, this just might be wishful thinking.

POLITICS, PANSIES AND PATRIOTISM

I would love to tell you that this dog yarn is over and done with, but mon père has been exposing me to toxic radiation on the boob tube spewed out by the dumber-than-dirt two-legged men and one dumbass harlot O'Hara I never want to meet: the GOP candidates running for the job of President of the United States of America. If one more two-legged ever talks down to me or any of my four-legged friends again, we are going to take a monster bite out of these cluck-suckers. My eyes roll in my wire fox sockets when any one of these morons lets loose on what is supposed to be reason to elect him (or her) Commander-in-Chief. "Hail, Mary, full of grace…"

By the time you read this probably one of these hyenas will have been chosen to represent, er…, misrepresent the GOP in the General Election in November. And then again, stay tuned for a fractured, gun-slinging Republican Convention. Abraham Lincoln, reputed to be the greatest two-legs ever to be president of the Republic, was a Republican. Yea, ladies and gentlemen of the Jury, but he freed the slaves. This group of Grand Ole Party cracker jacks seem to want to put a lot of folks back in chains.

For starters, mankind can thank God from whom all blessings flow that three of the billy goats and one nervous-nelly goat decided to drop out of the race for the White House. I am talking about Rick Perry and Herman Cain, that dim bulb, Mr. Huntsman and Michelle Whoever who finally dropped her high-heel climb because she ran out of money and Tea Partiers.

As I watched those painfully stupid debates, Rickella Perry couldn't remember who he was or what he believed in. It was like watching a third grader being stumped over a simple question about what three departments of the government he would get rid of. When he stutter-stepped trying to conger up an answer, I nearly swallowed a treat whole when he whispered "Oops" with a shit-eating grin on his stupid puss. It reminded me of Forrest Gump espousing one of his corny homilies about life in the deep South. Miss Perry doesn't know how old a hay seed has to be to cast a vote. Hell, I even know I'm too young to put a paw print on a ballot, but not brain-freeze Perry. Rick Perry's blue jeans are so tight he needs a boyfriend. God, are we done yet?

About shuckin' and jivin' Herman Cain I will only say thank God Cain's womanizing got him kicked to the curb. Mon père wrote President Obama a letter saying he was the reincarnation of Abraham Lincoln. Dada was pissed off that nobody called him to come to the White House or revealed that to the Great Unwashed — but he and I are still going to vote for the reincarnation of the greatest president who ever lived. Herman Cain is a retread of Minnesota Fats peddling snake oil. Although Cain really concocts a mean pizza, he would rather cook up a moon pie. Well I was going to ramrod his big ass butt with my terrier backside until he begged, "Stop the gravy train I want to get off of this Streetcar named Desire!" And sure enough, he was gone with the wind.

As far as Mr. Huntsman is concerned, I call him Whispering Smith because he makes you think that he stumbled onto the stage not knowing that he had come to beg to be President of the United States of America. Maybe he knew enough mostly to keep his yapper shut. For my two-cent's worth, have we seen the last of him? Just asking.

The Tea Party is about to swallow after pouring all that checkerberry that the GOP has been brewing since Reconstruction. As far as Chris Matthews and I are concerned, the GOP train will leave the station without having chosen an electable candidate. As my editor says, tell your readers to stay tuned because we have to get my new book to the printer. From my view from our comfy Pretesi-sheeted bed, it seems as if the transits in the sky, aka astrological forecasting, indicate that the GOP is going to have a hard time picking the lesser of two evils.

A RAMBLIN' RECKLESS REPUBLICAN RECRUIT

My publishers had to hold the presses because that slick, narcissistic cracker-jack from Pennsylvania who lost his senate seat a few years ago, Rick Santorum, is the latest elephant to stampede to the front of the last man standing, Mitt Romney. I cracked open Rick Santorum's astrological birth chart file. Your eyes will bulge out of your heads when you read what I found out.

For starters, Sanitarium has the profile of a demagogue. Venus and Mercury in Aries — it's his way or no way at all. These aspects have dictator written all over them. His sun sign is Taurus, square his Moon in Aquarius. Even the lamest of you know what bulls do: Stampede! Ever watch the running of the toro in Pamplona, Spain during the San Fermin Festival? Got the picture? Dictator Sanitarium acting on mad impulse across America. Remember other political personalities throughout history started out with a platform to unseat the incumbent that turned out to be irrefutable unquestionable but illegal laws of the land?

He is a Catholic who disses homosexuals, contraception, abortions and anything else his Eminence wants to orate about. The thud heard 'round the world recently was Foster Friess, one of Ricky's biggest backers, telling the doyenne of truth-telling on MSNBC's Andrea Mitchell Reports the following:

"This contraceptive thing, my gosh, it's so... inexpensive. Back in my days, they used Bayer aspirin for contraceptives. The gals put it between their knees, and it wasn't that costly."

Ricky Sanitarium's response was "Hee haw, Deep Friess was joking." I guess Cheap Trick Rick thinks he and his posse are on Saturday Night Live. The joke is on them. When November rolls around this Great Pretender, the skulking savior and Genghis Khan of the almost-Late, Great Planet Earth is going to find himself back in Pennsylvania in a tent meeting wondering where the White House went. There were 6% more women than men who voted in 2008, and they are going to remember who denigrated them one more time. I keep barking to the Great Unwashed that it's a woman's world and nobody will listen except women who will decide who is the next President of these United States.

CALLING BILL MAHER! CALLING BILL MAHER!

I asked mon père if we could call Bill Maher on the phone. He said he didn't know his number. I was shocked since he usually has everybody's number. I bet Bill would stir the nest until there was just room enough for a new robin or two with a high I.Q. We watched his 'stand up and be counted' TV show one night. He was so out there, but I could still follow his drift. Mr. Darby can track him like a big-bellied Texan looking for black gold. Bill Maher for president! Bill Maher for president! (Dada just told me to pipe down; the next door neighbors living in sin are dyed wolves-in-sheep's-clothing Republicans). Bill Maher talks so fast and he's so smart I wondered if he was really two-legged — he can out-talk, out-walk and out-think the graduating class at Mensa. Maher throws the f-word around like it's his first language. If I get on his show I'll get a yap or bark in before the censors railroad me out.

Did you happen to read the story in cyberspace "Why Mitt Romney's Dog Is Getting A Lot Of Press?" I'll bet my last dog biscuit and a year's worth of spa treatments that all canines and dog lovers will chase his candy-ass rear-end back to the high rent district in Massachusetts where he used to be Governor. It seems that the Romneys were going on a long family vacation from Boston to Canada back in 2007 and Mitt tied his Irish Setter Seamus in his crate to the top of the station wagon. When he was asked about the questionable placement of the pooch, Romney said, "My dog loves fresh air." Even we four-leggeds stutter when we meet total insanity, but when it comes from the actions and out of the mouth of someone running for President of the United States, I want to stage a shit-in with a million barking and baying dogs to let this PETA-hated Republican know what we think of him and animal cruelty.

Before I get off politics, I gotta bark and yelp a little bit about Rachel Maddow. Dada and I think she's the smartest observer of the skewered political landscape of all the talking heads on television. One night we saw her chasing down one of the GOP candidates to get his comment about a dozen mistakes he'd made in one of the debates. He ran from her like she had a butcher knife and was about to carve and quarter him. We roar when she dresses up in a costume to dramatize a point. Our favorite part is when she plays back tape of what a candidate really said as opposed to what he wants you to believe he said. Rachel is feisty and relentless about getting to the bottom of something. Rachel sits ringside like a momma hen with six roosters and holds court. While they cock-a-doodle-do, she feathers the nest with bulls-eye facts and not fiction. Mon père says you can tell when this arbiter of what's left and what's right and where the middle is when she tilts her head and then does one of those Nikki Fink (for those of you who do not know who is the doyenne of all things Hollywood, google Nikki Fink and you'll never stop reading Deadline Hollywood) GOTCHA. Ya gotta love Rachel Maddow. If you want the truth and nothing but the truth about who believes what, but better yet, what they've done or haven't said that they said they did. Rachel, as Miss Oprah would say, you go girl!

Until I care enough to weigh in, I will leave you with these canine woofs of wisdom, "Don't look down on us four-leggeds because if you piss us off bad enough, particularly if you are a Republican, we'll tee tee on your leg, or worse."

THE CELESTINE PROPHECY COMES VISITING

Lo and behold, just when I thought I was the No. 1 canine in this house, Mr. and Mrs. Celestine Prophecy, James and Salle Redfield come knocking at our door—with a tiny white fluffy four-legged creature named Toby. They came in the side gate and the minute he opened his yapper to bark and take over the biggest and best backyard in the Village I knew I was going to be the outsider. His majesty opened the sliding glass door and Scott and Alison and the twins all made a bee-line for the Redfields and Toby. Guess who got left outside? Yeah, me. They left the screen door open so I could hear all the two-leg laying-on of ohs and ahs like they hadn't seen each other in two lifetimes. Truth be told, mon père had dinner with them in the Magic City, Birmingham four months ago.

Salle loves little tykes so much she brought them each a little white lamb. Alison nearly wet herself with glee as she had just tried to buy Augusta one because il principe had given Livia one just like it last Easter. You would have thought the girls were in an amusement park with the real Bugs Bunny they were so over the top deliriously ecstatic. Salle had gotten me a yummy big treat shaped like a bone which made me fume a little less from being stuck in the backyard.

For those of you who've been living under a rock, James Redfield wrote the biggest best seller in the history of spiritual books, The Celestine Prophecy in 1994. His latest epistle is The Twelfth Insight. Man, does that dude ever do anything but write? Oh, I forgot, he is a scratch golfer. Did I tell you that Dada has lived on this golf course more than 20 years and has never played a round of golf. Maybe he and the Redfields could swap houses and he and Toby could hunker down in Dixie and Momma and Papa Redfield could take care of me and he could play golf every day. I know, I know. I'm dreaming again. Why not. Both James and Mister G preach 'All things are possible.' Right. Tell that to a four-legged dog with peerage who has been sentenced to the backyard while some upstart takes over the Great Room in his own casa.

THINGS ARE NOT WHAT THEY SEEM

I have to wrap this up until my fan base begs for more words of wisdom. In the meantime, you know where to find me on Twitter or my Facebook page. E-mail me. I'll answer. I promise. And if you see me out and about, give me a yummy treat and we can talk and play and exchange recipes.

When we were on our morning walk today Dada told me that he is negotiating with a magazine for my own weekly column, From The Dog's Mouth. He said the editor wondered whether I had anything to say that would interest his two-legged readers. Geez, now do I have to put up with a lot of bullsh*t from a big piece of stuff from the Fourth Estate? We have to meet with him in a few weeks. If he digs my bow-wows and arfs the pay check can keep me in more treats than Jesse and my other four-legged pals and I can eat. I will put my paw prints all over his magazine.

Daddy tells me when we are alone at night before he turns out the light how he was raised in what seemed like a war zone. Too bad he couldn't have traded places with me and had to fight for momma's dugs (Wikipedia will tell you that this is a momma dog's mammary glands from which we pups suckle) to get our share of the milk of canine kindness. But I let him know that he and I have the best of everything we could ever want.

But before he channels George Burn's line to Gracie Allen (that star-power comedy team in the 50's and 60's with their own television show — I know because il principe makes us watch them on classic reels time to time), "Say, 'good-night,' Mr. Darby," I want to let you know that things are never ever what they seem.

Case in point, my keeper thought I was coming to Sedona so he could save me from the rubes in Iowa. Stinking thinking, as he likes to crow to the Great Unwashed. No way, Jose and Antoinella, did I come to the Grand Canyon state, running from what he thinks are country bumpkins. I took the Lewis and Clark trail over here in order to open him up to the great limitless untapped inner riches that could make his face for the world to see happier and more open-minded. Did he learn this lesson? In spades.

The second most important unwritten rule of civility we discovered was that "he who teaches learns." What he and I do with what we uncover is the bottom line of why he and I were put together by the Big Magnet in the Sky —spirit guides. (We all have them, you know?). That is indelible and irrevocable for both two-leg and four-legs. Remember when he said, "Eat," and I told him "When I'm hungry?" Will you ever get it through your head that a dog does not poo on command and that we four-leggeds are not here to wear all the latest get-ups to make our human companions show us off to their friends and neighbors? We do not do Halloween and we have no interest in making a fashion statement. Human beings would have a lot more money in their treasure chests if they saved more than they spent.

And I have one more zinger I want to leave with you before I get the call to continue to throw out my opinions on all subjects — no off-limits for me — for that magazine for the rich and ridiculous. Love should never come with a price. Two- and four-legs can have the best relationship in the world if canines are not controlled, mistreated or taken for granted. The one thing that will send us four-legs looking for higher ground is abuse, physical, emotional or spiritual. Daddy never abused me. Rather, he tried to exercise wrong use of will with me. And in time it all worked out for both him and me. The lesson here is to listen more than you yaketty-yak-yak. The treasured times of your life with your gift from God will come when you look into each other's eyes and mirror love and affection that comes from your deepest wells.

Dada's deepest darkest secret is that he wishes he had been an actor. (One of his clients, a Tony Award-winning producer told him once, 'We are all in show business.' He's right, you know).

I will now use the tag line of one of his favorite characters from the silver screen, Jimmie Durante, to say to one and all, two legs as well as four, so long, for now. "Good-night, Mrs. Calasbash, wherever you are."

11

ACKNOWLEDGEMENTS

I would never have put a paw to paper had it not been for Gail Bell and Andrew Bell aka The Kid. Gail has had a lot of Wire Fox Terriers in her life so she knew how to tell mon père to pipe down when he thought I was his problem.

And The Kid may be two-legged but he sure as the dickens (an expression that was first used in The Merry Wives of Windsor by Shakespeare) knows how to talk my language. Kid is responsible for how far and wide my book has traveled. His think tank has so many brilliant ideas whoever hires him will be getting a genius. He twitters for me since my paws keep making a mess of the messages. This young tennis champion conjures outside the box of boredom and his vivid imagination creates ways in which the world can hit the BUY ME button for *From the Dog's Mouth* on book seller sites. But I want to thank him most of all for being my BFF and having the courage to tell Dada that I have room enough for a lot more two-leggeds in my life than just Daddy. To quote Scott Carney, "You're the Kid, Kid!"

To Chao Liao goes high praise for steering this book away from big pieces of stuff agents (in their own mind, at least). Hip hip hooray to Mr. Beijing for keeping it away from the jaundiced opinions of the pantheon of mainstream publishing and ushering it right into the game plan of the all-seeing, all-knowing experts at FastPencil, the 21st century alternative to the pain and suffering of the hoi polloi of Guttenberg's successors. A 12-gun salute to this genius technocrat whom il principe, my keeper (some refer to him as the latter-day Nostradamus) says is the smartest man in the world. Praise God from whom all blessings flow.

Although I only know her from a distance, I would like to thank Karin Price Mueller, the mother of three brilliant children and two four-legged gifts to her household and the wife of one journalist husband, for the smooth as silk manuscript, its organization, all ironed out syntax and alternative choices of how to better express myself. As usual Dada is leaving me home when he flies off to New York for his birthday, to see clients and to schmooze with Karin. Bless her house and thank God mon père turned me and my book over to her smart sense of how much better this book became.

I want to give big wet licks and kisses to Scott, Alison and Livia and Augusta for helping me settle Daddy down the hundreds of times he wanted to send me back to Iowa. Scott is the brightest bulb in any bunch Daddy ever knew—he challenged my keeper to learn from me as I needed to look at my options for minding Dada. And a thousand bark-salute to Alison who is as staunch and determined as the pyramids. Don't mess with Texas or big-alieck, as she is know in cyberspace. I will keep giving up my treat and toy money to make sure the twins have a hefty dowry when they grow up and marry blueblood princes. And while I am at it, I understand why you let someone else raise Riggs. The deal worked better for you and for him.

To Riggs, wherever you are, thanks for being my best friend and giving me the best two years of my life. I may meet a lot of four-leggeds, big and small, mild and mean, but none will ever replace the canine who taught me to stand up for myself and to play fair with a brother from a different mother.

To Linda, who worked for Scott and mon père and who was good to me every day she was here, and to Danni who replaced her, and who is a great companion when I need her, Grazie mille as the Italians say.

But most of all I need to give a gold medal to Mister G who wrote exactly as I told him to, even when it did not cast him in the best light in the play he wrote us both into. He taught me that there is no perfect and that two days are never the same—just 24 hours with another set of challenges with another chance to get it right.

Although they are new to the collaboration I already love Bruce Butterfield a big piece of stuff at my publisher FastPencil—and who has a great long-haired dachshund named Danny whom I hope to meet on The View. His contracts are crisp and fair. Mariena Foley has a chart that makes me slobber with ecstasy. She has four planets in Sagittarius on top of my Moon. Wait'll we meet. She might be the momma I've been waiting for as long as I've lived with mon père. I would be remiss if I didn't throw a few kudos to Matt O'Leary without whom this book would not have had the best come-and-read-me cover imaginable and a perfect stylized chapter format that lets you glide through my prose. One thing I know. My spirit guides tell me that my masterpiece is in the right hands.

And a lot of arfs and yaps to all who buy this book. If enough of you like it I just may write another one. As they say on television when there is more to come, stay tuned.

My name is Mr. Darby, and I approve of these acknowledgements.

12

MR. DARBY'S FRIENDS

MR. DARBY'S TWO-LEGGED FRIENDS

Augusta and Livia Carney are anxious to read Mr. Darby's new book FROM THE DOG'S MOUTH

Mister G. and Mr. Darby with their Best Friends, Scott and Riggs, a Red Heeler Australian Shepherd mix. "Those were the days!"

"Augusta and Livia Carney, one of ya'll make room so Mr. Darby can ride with you." Augusta is in blue and Livia is in pink.

"Mr. Darby ate all my cheerios, daddy." Augusta Carney ponders whether there's any more in the box.

"Momma, can we take Big Hairy home with us? Why not?"

This was Riggs' family & my best friends, Alison and Scott Carney, and gorgeous geniuses, Livia and Augusta.

Kate Friedman Lourie with two of the four-legged friends she loves most.

"Anybody wanna boogie-woogie?" Livia Carney could make Scrooge laugh and a grouch less grumpy.

The Bells, who Mr. Darby considers his First Family: beautiful Gail, the tennis champ Kid Bell and the world's top chef, David.

Two of the world's smartest men, Andrew Bell and Chao Liao at Trinity College graduation May 2011.

Chao Liao and Kid Bell outside the Great Hall of the People in Beijing, China. If they can't make the world a better place, no one can.

Dada has a bet that nobody can guess the age of Carole Marcus Pizitz. He said she is as beautiful as the day he met her umpteen years ago.

Kid Bell, aka Andrew Joseph, who Mr. Darby thinks will one day be President of the United States and his sister, the diva and soul of song, Ashley Galvani Bell, who will debut at the Met and La Scala, sooner than later.

Birmingham's beautiful angel, Carole Marcus Pizitz and her big-hearted husband, Michael Pizitz. They painted their philanthropic emporium, Gus Meyer pink to honor Breast Cancer Awareness in Birmingham in 2011.

A Gathering, Pizitz, Seltzer and Grey Clans in Gus Meyer, the South's fashion store extraordinaire. Jason Seltzer and Carole's daughter Stephanie Seltzer, their daughter Kate and son, Dean, Carole and Michael Pizitz, Jaden Grey, Carole's daughter Robin.

The Colorado Crowd, Robin and her husband Chris Grey and their brilliant son Jaden.

Miss Israel Civil Rights, Birmingham Person of the Year, Cathy Ovson Friedman. Nobody gives more than she does to both two-legged and four-legged causes.

Talia, Lila and Ava Fleisig and Momma Julie Friedman Fleisig. Dada and I think of these girls as Momma Rose's (aka Cathy Friedman) dancers and singers headed for Broadway.

Paul and Cathy Friedman checking out the vibes in Red Rock Country Sedona, the Mecca of the Southwest.

Kate Friedman Lourie, her niece Talia Fleisig and husband Josh Lourie. Kate took mon pere to school as Show 'N Tell when she was a young kid. Oy vey!

My Dada and I call the Bells First Family because they are the nicest people we know. If their Wire Fox Terrier Curtsey would share her bed I'd go home with them in a Miami minute. Here they are, when the world was younger.

Ladies and gentlemen, four-leggeds as well, here is Mr. Darby's favorite woman in the world, Gail Galvani Bell. GRRRRR.

MR. DARBY'S FOUR-LEGGED FRIENDS

This beautiful snow-white little lady flew off to Heaven last year. She sends good vibes to Mr. Darby and all four-legged friends on Earth—Annie, A Maltese from Sedona, Arizona.

"Just like most Wire Fox Terriers I am spirited, full of tricks and surprises and too much fun to be around. Just like handsome headstrong Mr. Darby. My name is Babe Steele Powell. But I am affectionately know as Bebe"—from New York and Palm Beach.

"Though I'm only 4-months-old & already more than 3X Mr. Darby's weight, I already look up to this guy. I hope the wisdom he imparts to all two-legs spreads far and wide. Buddha — English Mastiff, New Jersey

"My mommy and I are waiting, Mr. Darby, for our autographed copy of your new book. I hear it is fabulous." Curtsey and mommy Gail Bell in their Southampton manse

"I've got my eyes on you, Mr. Darby. Watch your p's and q's around my house, big guy!"—Curtsey, a champion Wire Fox Terrier from New York, Southampton and Sedona.

"Dada, don't be mad at me but I just did a poo on your million-dollar Persian rug. I couldn't reach the handle on the door to let myself out." —Mr. Darby, seven months old.

"Best wishes for success with your book, Mr. Darby. It's about time we got a four-legged perspective on all of those two-legged issues" -Honeybear, a Yorkiepoo from Sedona, Arizona

"Jesse, you might as well give up. You are playing in my yard with my rules. Let go. I win."

"Turn around, little brother Jesse, it's time for your close-up."

Mr. Darby just wrangled his favorite toy away from his younger brother, Jesse.

Mister G. and Mr. Darby and his brother Jesse. Betcha can't tell which is which. Same mother from a different litter.

This is Mr. Darby's first play-date with his brother Jesse.

"Mr. Darby is a gentleman and a scholar and I am proud to call him friend. He welcomed me with open paws when I visited him in Sedona and I always look forward to our enlightening encounters." - Joe Noonan - Venice, California

"I really like Mr. Darby. He looks smart and funny, and he has witty observations. Please read this book and perhaps Mr. Darby can teach you a thing or two! Woof" - Lulu Lebovitz, a Shih Tzu from Sedona, AZ and Los Angeles, CA.

"I am a female nearly fully-grown English Mastiff, I took one look at Mr. Darby's photo and wanted to eat him up. Then when my momma read to me from his book, WOW! I must declare that his words are even more delicious than he is." —Mojo from New Jersey

"Come, Mr. Darby and join me in meditation. It will be good for your Wire Fox Terrier soul." - Motte Manigault, a King Charles Spaniel who lives in Charleston, SC.

"My name is Savannah Shinn. Mr. Darby is my next-door neighbor. When I found out he had written a book I wanted to endorse it. Woof. Woof." Savannah Shinn, a Shih Tzu from Sedona, Arizona

MR. DARBY AND RIGGS, HIS BEST FRIEND

Riggs, Mr. Darby's Best four-legged Friend, when he was three months old.

Riggs had those "I am watching your every move, Mr. Darby" beady eyes when he was just a puppy.

Riggs grew up to be a loving and brave dog, and always Mr. Darby's favorite pal at work and at play. He still misses him every day.

Riggs was rescued by the Human Society of Sedona and lived with the Carneys until he was three years-old.

"Who just jumped into my warm bed?" Riggs had his eyes on Mr. Darby at all times. At least until his friend fell asleep.

Brothers with different mothers—Mr. Darby and Riggs, his BFF. There will never be another twosome like these four-legged friends.

"Mr. Darby, this is my favorite bone. Drop it!"